GCRAP

LEAD YOURSELF FIRST. BOUNCE BACK.
GET SH*T DONE

CHARLES "CHIP" LUTZ, MSED, CSP
Lieutenant Commander, United States Navy *(Retired)*

Copyright @ 2017 by Charles Lutz. All rights reserved.

Thank you for buying an authorized edition of this book and for complying with copyright laws.

You are respectfully entrusted to not reproduce, scan, distribute, transmit or record any part herein without prior permission, with the exception of brief quotations embodied in critical reviews and certain other noncommercial uses permitted by copyright law.

This publication contains material for educational purposes only. The author and publisher have made every effort to ensure that the information in this book was correct at press time and do not assume and hereby disclaim any liability to any party for any loss, damage, or disruption caused by errors and omissions.

GET PAST THE CRAP! Lead Yourself First, Bounce Back, Get Sh*t Done
by Charles Lutz

Cover & Interior Design by Kendra Cagle, www.5LakesDesign.com

ISBN-10: 978-1981539642
ISBN-13: 1981539646

www.unconventionalleader.com

DEDICATION

This book is dedicated to all the people and situations that have caused crap in my life. I wouldn't be who I am without having gone through it.

CONTENTS

CHAPTER 1 | Got Crap? **PICK OPTION 3** *1*

CHAPTER 2 | Get Past the Crap with **PURPOSE** *23*

CHAPTER 3 | Get Past the Crap by being a
POSITIVE THINKER *41*

CHAPTER 4 | Get Past the Crap by **PAYING ATTENTION** *59*

CHAPTER 5 | Get Past the Crap by being **PLIABLE** *77*

CHAPTER 6 | Get Past the Crap with **PRACTICE** *95*

CHAPTER 7 | Get Past the Crap with **PLAY** *111*

CHAPTER 8 | Get Past the Crap by **TAKING THE PLEDGE** . . . *131*

CHAPTER 9 | Putting It All **TOGETHER** *145*

Acknowledgments *149*

About the Author. *151*

CHAPTER 1

GOT CRAP?
PICK OPTION 3

"In any moment of decision, the best thing you can do is the right thing. The worst thing you can do is nothing."
–Theodore Roosevelt

It was Easter 2017. I was up early to go the sunrise service at church with my mom and was feeling pretty good after four days of feeling really crappy. On the previous Wednesday, very suddenly, I started having sharp pains in my abdomen. The pain got progressively worse as the morning went on and became so uncomfortable that I had trouble walking. I told my lovely bride, Gwen, that we needed to go to the Emergency Room.

Now, I'm not one to even go to the doctor's office. I think a lot of us guys are like that. I view every medical issue as a minor hiccup to be dealt with later. I've still not gotten the shoulder surgery that I was supposed to get when I retired from the Navy a decade ago. I figure I'll have time for that later. However, this felt a little more urgent.

2   Get Past The Crap

During the 20-minute drive to the ER, I felt every bump in the road as if a wicked little child was stabbing me in the gut with a sharp stick. When we arrived at the hospital, I luckily got in to see the doctor right away as the piercing pain continued to get worse.

After several hours of poking, prodding, and pensive looks, I was diagnosed with diverticulitis. I had never heard of this before but, as Google would later reveal, it is common and with antibiotics could be taken care of fairly easily. I like easy. The worse part was that the antibiotics were the kind that had a severe adverse reaction when mixed with alcohol. That meant that the vodka tonic I had been looking forward to all day while hanging out in the ER was now off the table, literally.

This was a bad time to be sick. I guess there is never a good time to fall ill, but I had a lot to do. I had a speaking engagement coming up and my two youngest children were shipping off to Navy boot camp (in their ol' man's footsteps) and I was the host for their going-away party. There was food to make, cleaning to be done, and plenty of stuff that needed my attention.

Gwen urged me to postpone the party or, at the very least, move it to a different location. I wouldn't have it. This was the last time these two kids would call this their home and I really wanted them to have a good memory of their send-off. If they had nothing else to think about while being socialized into military life, I wanted them to at least think of all their friends and family gathered to see them go.

The next three days were jam-packed with the aforementioned activities and it was nearly party time! The event was made even more special since my 80-year-old mother drove up to join us for the festivities. She has always been close to my kids, probably because I'm her favorite child. (All my siblings say that, but my money's still on me as the favorite.)

My appetite had been non-existent since the ER visit. I hadn't eaten much at all those last couple days…especially the Saturday of the party as I was too busy. Finally, when able to take a break from preparations, I poured myself an extra-large iced tea (that wished it was a vodka tonic) and pulled out the pepper jack cheese.

Looking cautiously at me, my mother asked, "Do you think you should be eating that?"

"What's going to happen?" I responded with a shrug.

Little did I know at that time how those words would come back to haunt me.

While on my second cup of coffee the next morning, Easter Sunday, all hell broke loose inside my body. I didn't know what was happening. I started shaking uncontrollably and sweating in places I didn't know I could sweat. I knew another trip to the ER was inevitable. I crawled into the bedroom where my wife lay sleeping so soundly.

"Gwen…Gwen…" My voice shook as I tried to get her name out. She looked at me, confused, as to why I was waking her before the chickens were even up. "We have to go to the hospital. Now."

There are many reasons I fell in love with Gwen. She's a farm girl. One minute she's out knee deep in horse shit and the next minute she can look like a movie star. She can also, in an emergency, be ready quick. Please note that I said, "in an emergency." Other times, not so much.

Gwen sprung out of bed, grabbed my mom and we were off to the ER for another visit.

I still felt each bump of the drive but instead of a child with a stick stabbing me, this time it felt like a flaming hot sword going through my midsection. When we got to the hospital, the pain in my abdomen was excruciating. I have a high tolerance for pain but I was in tears. I just wanted it to stop.

One problem with ERs is that you rarely see the same medical staff, especially on a holiday, and you end up having to repeat everything (several times) as you try to explain that you think you're dying and you just want them to put you to sleep.

After describing (multiple times) what I was feeling and a series of tests that were very much like the ones I had the Wednesday prior, the last words I remember before waking up ten hours later are, "Mr. Lutz, you have a perforated bowel and we need to do surgery."

In case you're up for it, here's the medical diagnosis for a perforated bowel:

> "A perforated bowel is a medical emergency in which a hole in the bowel opens to allow its contents to empty into the rest of the abdominal cavity. The result is frequently sepsis or blood infection, which if not treated can cause almost immediate death. A perforated bowel can occur as the result of traumatic injury, Crohn's Disease, or diverticulitis."

Immediate death?! What the hell?! I was not even yet 50 years old. Why would my body mutiny like this? I've always been good to it. Okay, maybe not good. But I have always ensured it's had enough donuts, red meat, and alcohol.

Even though my mom was certain that it was the pepper jack cheese that caused this explosion in my bowels, it was most definitely the diverticulitis that was the culprit (the pepper jack probably didn't help). Why didn't they tell me this could happen?

This wasn't a good time for surgery. It was a holiday, my kids were leaving, and I had work to do. This blowing-apart of my schedule (and my body) was crap! Not only due to the literal crap that was floating around within my body due to the perforated bowel, it was a crappy situation that I now had to deal with and didn't have time for. It was a big crap sandwich that I had to get past in order to get on with living and to make a living!

The next thing I knew, I was waking up in the elevator after surgery, staring pensively at a man standing over me. I read his name tag. It said, "Dale." With crackled voice, I pointed at the name tag and said his name. I then pointed at myself and said my name, "Chip."

I pointed back and forth between us repeating, "Chip….Dale….. Chip…..Dale…" I then said, "We should go on the road." Dale looked at me quizzically and ignored this awesome attempt at post-surgery humor. I fell back asleep. Hopefully with a smile on my face.

Waking up again in my hospital room surrounded by my wife, my mother, and my children, I must've looked like hell because they all gazed at me with a mixture of pity and horror. Thankfully, I was feeling pretty good. The drugs they gave me were some good shit! My glance shifted to each of my kids. I've always told my darling children that if I ever got to a place later in life where I didn't know who I was and couldn't take care of myself, one of them had to promise to smother me with a pillow. Each of them said they couldn't do it (even though they knew I said it in jest) except for my son, Christian. He said he would do it with this caveat…he wanted it in writing that it was okay.

I looked up at the ceiling and said, "Christian…..Christian!" (in my saddest, sickest voice). "Get the pillow."

He sheepishly smiled (knowing full well what I meant). I think, even though I looked like death, that helped him (and everyone else in the room) feel a little better.

This book is hopefully going to make you feel a little better.

We all have our crap to deal with. Hopefully yours is not so literal, but it's all very real. As the proverbial bumper sticker says, SHIT HAPPENS. Sometimes it seems that life is all just a bunch of crap. From the people we have to work with or for, to office politics, to strained relationships at home, and to the world at large, it can feel like the steaming hot crap sandwich gets served up to us all the time. And we all have to get past it. That is the reason for this book. Nobody enjoys crap. (If you don't even like the word, you might want to stop reading now because "crap" gets said a lot.) Like it or not, we all know crap is a part of life.

You are not alone when you face the crap, and here's the deal: you can learn some tactics to be more resilient and be a better leader, no matter what is going on in your life. You can face the day with less stress and a healthier perspective to handle the challenges that come your way. Remember that leading others always begins with leading yourself and getting past your crap is a skill that always comes in handy. Like all skills, it can be learned.

You know you have to take the reins and lead yourself first. It would be nice if we could segment our leadership life from the rest, but that's just not the case. Why? Because we're human beings and whole people. We take ourselves with us everywhere we go. Crap has a way of sticking to your shoe and going with you everywhere.

But fear not. Even if it feels like your entire life is a series of crap sandwiches, you CAN get past it and do the job that you need to do, personally and professionally. You are no good to your team as a leader if you're mired down by all the crap you have to deal with it, so tuck in that napkin under your chin and get ready to pick up that sandwich.

AS YOU KNOW, CRAP COMES AT US FROM ALL PLACES.

Work

I've worked with some great people in my life, and I've also worked with some crappy ones. Not just bosses. Boss crap is easy to focus in on (and we all have a boss) because the boss is the one that usually holds your career in their nasty, sweaty palms. But you have worked with the crappy co-worker too. You know the one: the guy or gal who makes work life intolerable for you and everyone around them. It could be their work ethic that makes them crappy, or maybe it's the fact that their brownnosing is so real you can smell the boss's crap on their face. (Too graphic? Sorry.) Regardless, they suck to work with and can impact you and your team. For me, the crappiest people to work with are the ones with the bad attitudes.

Maybe for you it's not the people; maybe it's the type of work you have to do that is crappy. I've been there too. Perhaps you've been put on a task with no rhyme or reason why this effort even needs to be done or why it's on your plate. Work crap can seem never-ending. It is exhausting to even think about all the past crap I've had to do (including cleaning up real crap in the head as a junior Sailor). No matter where you work or what you do, we all face crap in some way, shape, or form from time to time (or all the time) at work.

Home

We want home to be a haven and a respite from the problems we face at work, but when you walk in your door at the end of a long day, you can be met head-on with crap there, too. We had a saying in the Navy that your family didn't come in your seabag, meaning leave your home problems at home and don't bring them to work. Nice theory, but impossible in practical application. You can't separate yourself from your problems like that. It would be nice if we could, but that's just not the case. Problems at home creep into your work. That's life. And on the flip side, if you have problems at work, they often come home with you too.

I've got four children. I've got an ex-wife. When they had issues at home, it was crap I had to get past and still lead the team at work. No matter what your family life presents you, be it a broken toilet, kids' problems, or a broken marriage, that crap stays on your mind even though you still have to be present and on task at work. The truth is you can't leave the seabag anywhere; it's always with you. In these pages, I'll share how to lighten the load.

Health

From hernia surgeries, to chronic sinus infections, to having a perforated bowel and shitting in an ostomy bag for months

(TMI?), I know how poor health can be a crap sandwich. Sometimes it's not even your own health, but the health of a loved one that's the crap. I've been through that, too. No matter what or who, it's not pleasant but you've still got things to do, goals to be achieved and people to be led. Life keeps rolling, so we need to learn to roll with it, even while we are still rolling around in our crap. (Perhaps we can imagine pigs rolling around in the mud. They seem happy.)

You get the picture. (I've used the word "crap" at least thirty times already so yeah, that image is forming. You feel it.) Your own crap can come from anywhere, but those three above (work, home, and health) are the typical primary sources of our distress. We all have to deal with these stressful kinds of situations.

When the crap does come your way (and it will), you'll ask yourself, How did I get this sandwich and what am I supposed to do with it? That's why you are reading this book, to get the answers.

Regardless of the size, stench, or the origin of your sandwich, you have 3 options on how to deal with it.

....

OPTION 1:
TURN AWAY

Turning up your nose and walking away does absolutely nothing to take care of the sandwich you've been served. You can ignore it, but it's still there. As a matter of fact, the longer we let it sit on the table, the smellier, nastier, and more distasteful it becomes. Eventually, if left completely unattended, your crap sandwich will stink up your whole house, office, and life.

I've never had any good results from ignoring the problems in my life. They've only gotten worse. Thus, Option 1 isn't really a viable option at all.

A month prior to my perforated bowel I knew that something wasn't right, but I ignored my body and the signs it was trying to tell me. As usual, I kept the pace I always keep and turned my nose away from my instincts that something needed attention. What happened? A 10-inch incision in my abdomen and a week-long hospital stay. I ended up with a larger pile of crap than if I had just dealt with it in the beginning.

As with health issues, ignoring work problems doesn't make them go away. I couldn't totally ignore the crappy people I had to deal with every day at work, but I certainly tried to limit my exposure to them. They still affected me and my ability to work effectively. Further, the more you turn a blind eye to problem behavior of staff or colleagues, the more it becomes "acceptable" behavior and makes the crap worse.

Ignoring my ex-wife's affairs would have been nice. (And now you know why she is the ex-wife.) I would have preferred not to know about them at all, but that's not how life works. For the record, I realize that relationships take two people. I work. A lot. That's what I do…it's part of my DNA and sometimes I put work before everything else in my life (okay, I do that a lot). But, if you feel like you're not getting what you need from a relationship, tell the other person when you're feeling neglected. Don't go out and bang someone else. But I digress.

When my dad was diagnosed with Stage IV lung cancer, I wished I could have ignored that terrible crap sandwich. He was an idol to me and I had always looked at him as immortal. Him getting sick consumed my mind and impacted everything in my life. It certainly wasn't something that I could leave out of my seabag.

You get the idea. Life will always hand us some crap. You've got your own flavor and layers of the sandwich, but no matter what it is, walking away from the crap you're served does not solve the problem.

....

OPTION 2:
NIBBLE AND COMPLAIN

The nibble and complain option is miserable for everyone concerned. The sandwich certainly does not get more appetizing as it sits and oozes out onto the table. You are miserable because with every tiny bite, you remind yourself how much you hate this sandwich and how much you are going to loathe taking the next bite. The people around you are miserable because not only are they subjected to the smell, but they also have to listen to you whine about the taste and how terrible it is that you got served this sandwich.

Sure, they'll placate you and agree that it is awful that this crap got put in front of you, but there isn't one person in the vicinity of that foul stench that doesn't wish you would shut up and do something about it (even if they're ignoring or nibbling and complaining about their own crap sandwiches).

We've all heard that the easiest way to eat an elephant is one bite at a time. That is under the pretense that the elephant is a giant goal and you're taking on the elephant head on and taking action steps to get where you want to go. That's not what we're talking about with nibble and complaining. When you make the decision to nibble and complain, you ARE NOT taking the crap head on. You're being a wimpy mouse. Or a cry-baby three-year-old. You're half ignoring it, and half just pushing it around on the table hoping it will somehow go away. Guess what? It doesn't.

A few years ago, the bottom fell out of a huge speaking and training contract I had with the government. I didn't have enough eggs in other baskets and my cash flow was no longer flowing. The funny thing about money is that it might not make the world go around but, if you don't have any, the world doesn't stop. Bills still need to get paid. The timing of this contract fallout was freshly post-divorce. I had lawyer bills, I was paying a metric assload in child support (that's a Navy term for "a lot"), and dealing with my ex getting half of my military retirement. This surprise turn of events in my business left me up the proverbial shit creek without a paddle.

What did I do? I complained. I complained about the contract going south. I complained about my ex. I complained about creditors calling me. I nibbled and complained. I made myself and everyone around me miserable. What should I have been doing? Something. Anything. Something always nets something. Nothing nets nothing. Complaining nets nothing. I should have been taking Option 3.

OPTION 3:
TAKE A BIG BITE AND ASK FOR MORE

This option is all about tackling that sandwich "crust first" and not letting anything stand in your way in consuming every crumb. You aren't going to let the stink or the taste keep you from finishing every nasty little morsel. No, you aren't happy it got served to you but if you don't take care of it, who will? You can't send it to someone else to eat when it is yours alone to devour.

Option 3 is all about your attitude in taking care of this problem sandwich. If you couple that attitude with a rapid approach and steady effort, you'll have it consumed in no time. Sure, your stomach might ache a bit but you'll feel better for having tackled it and others will admire your iron constitution. This is the path of a champion and the one you want to use!

No matter what sandwich I've been served in my life, Option 3 has never served me wrong. You have to make the choice, the decision, to take it on and face the crap. The only way past it is through it.

When I found out about my ex's affairs, I took the sandwich on. I confronted her, the other parties, and my own role in the situation. I went head on trying to fix our relationship. Again, it takes two so you can only do so much, but I was better for facing it.

When my dad was ill, I went fully into trying to be there for him and my mom. This not only helped them keep their joy, it helped keep my attitude in check as well. I had no control over what was going on with him, all I could do was control how I was going to deal with it.

I've never felt bad about addressing a crappy person at work. Usually we feel rotten because we stew and wait. It feels better to do something. Even if it's a supervisor. I've had a lot of crappy supervisors and I'll explain in a later chapter on how dealing with them is better than holding it in. Face that crappy person head on.

For the first week of being sick, I sat around and felt sorry for myself, but that didn't accomplish anything. What did work was facing it head on. If I had to have an ostomy bag on my abdomen and keep living a regular life, I wanted to do it the best way I could. I talked to others that had gone through the same thing, I researched what options were out there, and I took a big bite.

What keeps us from taking Option 3? Fear. The fear of the unknown, the fear of failure, the fear of looking stupid...the list goes on and on. Fear is a bitch. So is worry for that matter. Both can immobilize us and push us towards options 1 or 2. But that still leaves you with the ever-present crap sandwich. Option 3 might seem a little scary but much less so than the repercussions of the other options.

Getting served "The Sandwich" isn't the end of the world nor will it be the last time it will get put in front of you. How we deal with the sandwich comes down to how we want to live our life. We can turn away or nibble and complain, but is that really living? Our own personal growth and progression comes through how we work through adversity and tough times, not how we sail through life when everything is sugarplums and lollipops. Regardless of how foul the crap smells and tastes right now, you will be stronger for having faced it. Personally and professionally, I have never had a time when picking Option 3 didn't benefit me and spur great things in my life.

No one is exempt. It doesn't matter your income level, education, status, power, or position. We all face the sandwich at one time or another. How we handle our crap makes all the difference. History is replete with people that have gotten served a big sandwich and decided to do something about it. Your future history can be the same. That's the point of this book: to help you keep moving forward and to help you get past your crap.

Life is cyclical. You sail along like a happy camper and then you hit a bump in the road. Life hands you crap. You deal with it (Option 3). You grow. And off you go on to great things. Then you get another serving. And you face it. You experience success, more growth, and great things. And so on. If you are visual (like me), this is how the cycle looks in life.

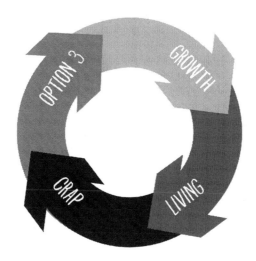

The key to a happier and less stressful life is not to deny that any crap will ever come your way, but to deal with it when it shows up with your name on it. This book is geared to prepare and encourage you. When you face your crap, you get past it. That's what effective leaders do. You make the choice to live well, be resilient, and not let the pile of poo weigh you down. You make the choice to get shit done!

I am not a psychologist, social worker, or scientist. I am is someone who uses the strategies I share here with you. They work.

All leadership is about leading yourself first. We learn best in the doing. This takes an active participation on your part. It's like anything: nothing works without work. It's like that time you heard a great speaker (Chip Lutz perhaps), then went home, got occupied with life, and didn't put anything the speaker said into practice. So what happened? Nothing. You maintained the status quo. No improvement. No growth.

You're better than that and you know it.

Decide right now. You have to WANT to get past the crap in your life. Option 3 may not always be easy or pretty but, in the end, you'll be better for it. You have to say...

"YES TO THE MESS AND NO TO THE STATUS QUO!"

If you don't want to make the choice to do something different to get past your crap, then please give this book to someone who does. I'm not kidding.

This material I provide in these pages is meant to be used. You will be asked at the end of each chapter to put the strategies to work for you.

Here's the practical application you'll be working through:

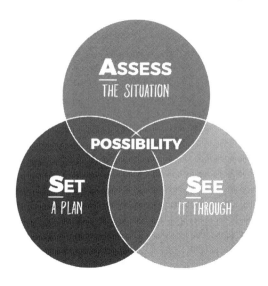

Assess the Situation. Set a Plan. See it Through. Okay, yes, the acronym spells ASS and, yes, I did that intentionally. It's easy to remember. ASS is about having a method for analyzing what crap is going on and having a method for getting past it. That's where the possibility happens.

Live from the place of what is POSSIBLE. I don't care about what's "probable." I know what's probable. It's probable that the sun is going to rise, it's going to set, and all of the crap is going to stay the same - - unless I take Option 3 and use this tool. That's what I'm about. I want to know what's possible. That takes work and it takes an understanding of where you're at in the world of crap.

Remember the last time you were at the doctor's office and they asked you where you were on the pain scale? They probably had an awesome little chart with differing levels and smile emojis for visuals. That's called a Visual Analogue Scale. It's helpful for everyone in breaking down the communication barriers that can arise when you're thinking one thing and the doctor is hearing another. Pain is relative to the person feeling it. So is the crap you've got to get past.

To help with the assessment of your crap pain, I've developed a **Visual Craptometer Scale.** Take a look:

VISUAL CRAPTOMETER SCALE

LEVEL 1	LEVEL 2	LEVEL 3	LEVEL 4
Everything is **CRAPTASTIC!**	Same Old **CRAP**	**CRAP** is getting **HEAVY**	My Life is **CRAP**
Good to go	Mild stress	Heavier stress	Depression
Prepared for daily events	Slightly anxious or irritable	Anger outbursts	Heavy anxiety
Relationships are intact	Some mood swings	Worrying/ losing sleep	No one enjoys being around you
Able to roll with daily crap	Daily grind is just that	Want to take a mental health day. Or a whole week	You think about disappearing to an island with no forwarding information

Similar to having one medical event that can catapult you to a different pain scale on the Visual Analogue Scale, the same is true with the crap in your life. All you need is one crappy life event to push you from a Level 1 to a 4. Taking Option 3 and actively employing the strategies can help move you to the next level. I will state, however, that if you're at a level 4 and the strategies aren't moving you, it's okay to get some professional help.

Take a look at the scale. Where do you say you are right now? Do you want to make a choice to lead yourself, bounce back and get shit done? Then let's get started!

CHAPTER 2

GET PAST THE CRAP WITH
PURPOSE

"The purpose of life is not to be happy. It is to be useful, to be honorable, to be compassionate, to have it make some difference that you have lived and lived well."

–**Ralph Waldo Emerson**

Resilient leaders have a purpose. It's larger than the purpose of just getting past the crap that is hitting you at the moment. Your purpose is the reason you get out of bed in the morning.

Purpose is what fuels your fire. It's what makes all the crap you have to get past worthwhile. Without a purpose, we're like ships without rudders, just drifting along with no real charted course. Any problem, issue, or challenge that gets thrown against us may push us in a different direction and that can cause even more crap to come our way.

But having a purpose keeps you on course. You deal with the circumstances that come up, and you do not get tossed about aimlessly in the crashing waves. It's important for you to find your special purpose. (Side note, the phrase "special purpose" reminds me of the classic movie comedy, The Jerk. Steve Martin's character Navin Johnson was so happy to find his "special purpose" that when he did, he immediately called his parents screaming, "I've found my special purpose!" Once you see or remember the movie you'll know his purpose was … a little different than what we're talking about here. But we still can emulate Navin's enthusiasm for finding our special purpose.)

My first two years in the Navy were purposeless. I wasn't stationed with people my own age or even on a ship. I got put in an office park with people that were old enough to be my parents. It sucked. Granted, I was a little obnoxious at age eighteen (not much has changed), but it was obvious that everyone I worked with was more concerned with curbing my wild streak than they were in tying me to purpose. I had daily tasks but I never knew why I did them or what their purpose was. Further, I didn't know what my purpose was. I felt like I was spinning my wheels going nowhere, a rudderless ship.

Every time crap came my way, I floundered and went in a different direction. I was unhappy and a bit testy and would, quite frankly, be the cause of a lot of extra crap that came my way. The stress and anxiety of each day would easily turn into a depressed slump and, at the end of the day, I'd go back to my barracks room and self-medicate with a drink (usually a Seagram's 7 and 7-Up). That was until Denny checked in and became my supervisor.

Denny wasn't that much older than me, just ten years but, in Navy years, he was seasoned and accomplished. Denny had taken the hard jobs in the Navy, done well at them, and was promoted quickly. I don't know if it was because he saw potential or a part of himself in me, but one day Denny decided to show me "the way."

Denny asked me, "Hey, Chip…do you want to make Chief in ten years like me?"

"Of course!" I answered. Wow, did he really think I could pull that off? I was intrigued!

Denny then listed all the things I needed to do to accomplish such a goal in that amount of time. That changed everything for me. Finally, someone saw more in me than a smartass young sailor. Not only that, I now had a purpose and a strategy, Denny's list, for me to get there.

Purpose and strategy are like peanut butter and jelly. Sure, you can have one without the other, but they work much better together. Having a purpose without some kind of strategy of how to go about fulfilling that purpose keeps you directionless. A purpose is the what and the strategy is the how.

Strategy 101 will tell you that any basic strategy is made up of three primary components:

1. A knowledge of where you are now.
2. A knowledge of where you want to go (purpose).
3. Some kind of path on how you are going to get there.

This purpose/strategy combination can do a lot to help you get past the crap that gets thrown at you on a daily basis.

First, purpose keeps you focused. Once Denny took me under his wing and helped me realize my purpose, I knew where I was going. I could answer any question, dilemma, or distraction that came up by filtering it through my purpose. Having a purpose kept me on task and on track. A good friend once told me, "Beware of distractions disguised as opportunities." Distractions can be a bunch of dung. If you're clear on your purpose, you are able to steer clear of distractions. You only need to ask yourself, "Does this 'opportunity' support where I am going?" If so, I'll do it. If not, I won't. That simple application dramatically reduces getting caught up in any distraction muck.

A PERSON CAN CONCENTRATE AND WORK ACTIVELY ONLY ON ONE OBJECT AT A TIME.

Think historically for a minute. Resilient leaders who accomplished great things were able to get past their crap because they were clear on their purpose and they let that be their guiding force.

George Washington was clear on his purpose on December 24th, 1776 when he decided that he needed to cross the Delaware River. 1776 had not been a good year for the Continental Army. Constant defeats had left the Army bare, deserting was the norm, and most of the men's time with the Army was soon coming to a close. Washington knew that he had to take drastic action to get past all that if he was going to fulfill his purpose. He did it and built the momentum needed to kick some ass even when circumstances were kicking his ass.

Martin Luther could have succumbed to all the crap he was getting from the Catholic church 500 years ago and not nailed his 95 theses to the door of a church. But, he was clear on his purpose and did it anyway. This example isn't about Protestants or Catholics or religion. It's just another example of purpose being a driver to get past your pile of poop. At that time the Catholic church was a powerhouse. They ruled people's lives and lorded over the princes of the land. Luther was so sure of his purpose he went up against excommunication, death threats, and poverty in order to fulfill his purpose.

General George Patton, one of the greatest military minds of all time, could have given in to the challenge of dyslexia and not pushed himself to learn how to learn and go to West Point, but he was clear on his purpose and pushed forward. World War II would have been a much different war if he had not been there. Patton was an ass kicking get-past-the-crap kind of leader. There are countless examples of people who have dealt with situations that may have seemed unsurmountable, but they pressed on because they were clear in their purpose. They chose Option 3 to take a bite and keep going, even if the going was pretty tough. Their success shows that Option 3 was the way to go.

You've got your own trials and tribulations you face. You could have given up reading this book already but you're clear on your purpose: to be able to get past your own crap and achieve great things.

Purpose also keeps you motivated and you'll need motivation to plow through the dingleberries that comes your way. That's not opinion, that's fact. (Well, maybe not the word dingleberries.) Sir Winston Churchill said, "When you're going through hell, keep on going." And Churchill knew about hell. Here was a guy that had gotten (basically) fired as Secretary of the British Navy for a tactical error during World War I, was humiliated and so he took an infantry job in the trenches to show what he was made of. He knew he was destined for greater things and rose up to be Prime Minister during World War II.

People throughout history have had to face horrific circumstances and events that we cannot even fathom. The service men who were prisoners in the Hanoi Hilton during the Vietnam War are one such example. I've read all their books and had the opportunity to talk to a couple of them on my podcast (www.leadershiphappyhour.com) to discuss their experiences.

It was purpose that got them through. Their purpose was to God, Country, and each other. They wanted to return with honor. Their experiences were nightmarish. They were tortured, beaten and, many times, isolated for years at a time. Yet these men, these resilient leaders, were able to get through each day because they kept their eye on the prize, the overall purpose for their lives.

That kind of motivation comes from having a long-range view that gives you the perspective that the crap o' the day is just one bump. We can get through today's challenges when we see the larger picture.

I was twenty-three years old and one year into my tour of duty at a Patrol Squadron and here I was at my desk, my head in my hands, sulking. Yes, sulking. I had just failed my 3-year job inspection and was beside myself with despair.

We had been working non-stop for the prior three months to make sure everything was in order prior to the inspector's arrival. The entire office had been putting in extra hours and we were sure that it would all go smoothly. It didn't. There were areas within my scope that I should have been doing that I didn't know about, and, ultimately, resulted in the failure.

I had never failed anything before. Okay, that's not true. I had failed but it was usually when I hadn't put in the work. This time, I did put in the work. I had walked the talk. I was ready and then…it was gone.

As I sat there (looking as pitiful as a dog that had just gotten reprimanded for getting into the trash), my Senior Chief walked in and asked, "What the hell is wrong with you, Lutz?"

I explained what had happened, my dismay, my despair, and returned to feeling sorry for myself. The Chief put his hand on my shoulder and said, "All in 20, Lutz."

"What the heck does that mean?" I asked.

"All in 20…all in 20 years. When you retire from the Navy, in 20 years, this isn't anything but one day, one setback, one hurdle that you'll go through. You'll face more but you'll also have triumphs along the way. Take the long-range view and quit feeling sorry for yourself. All in 20."

That's what I needed to give me the perspective to keep pressing on. The purpose that Denny and I had talked about five years earlier still motivated me. This incident was just one heaping mound of crap and all I needed to do was look past it and keep going, even if it felt like hell.

> **CRAPTASTIC FACT**
>
> FYI—"FAILURE" OFTEN LEADS TO INNOVATION AND TRANSFORMATION. THE INNOVATIVE COMPANY GOOGLE EVEN BUDGETS FOR FAILURE AND ITS POTENTIAL INSIGHT. GOOGLE EMPLOYEES ARE ALLOWED TO SPEND 20 PERCENT OF EACH WORKDAY ON THEIR OWN PROJECTS EVEN THOUGH 80 PERCENT OF GOOGLE VENTURES FAIL.

Purpose keeps you forward-thinking and helps you to not get stuck in a big puddle of was. Regrets suck. Getting stuck in yesterday, on how things used to be, doesn't keep you moving forward.

When I attended my 30-year high school reunion, I was amazed at how old everyone looked (except me, of course) and I was dismayed at how many were still stuck in that puddle of was and living in the past. It's great to remember glory days as a motivator, but we shouldn't reside there forever. Learn from the was and revel in it a bit. Take that with you, and focus on the now and what can be.

That event reminded me of a guy I used to work with. Ricky truly was a great guy. He was a genuinely nice person, and you knew there wasn't anything he wouldn't do for you. And yet, there wasn't anything Ricky was doing for himself.

He wasn't going anywhere. Ricky was like the rudderless ship, spinning in circles. He was always thinking about what could be, talking about it sometimes, but never taking any action. Ricky knew he had potential based on his past achievements, but the crap of life had beaten him down so much that he wasn't willing to take a new chance on anything and risk losing more (or having more crap come his way).

Fast forward three years in our work relationship, Ricky was still just thinking and talking about things. Same old, same old. He was in the puddle. Too many people stay there splashing around, but not having any fun and not working towards a purpose.

I'm sure you know people like Ricky. They have lots to offer but don't go for it. They keep their head down and stay stuck in the muck when just a little bit of effort could change everything.

> **CRAPTASTIC FACT**
>
> ACCORDING TO RESEARCH PUBLISHED IN PSYCHOLOGICAL SCIENCE, A JOURNAL OF THE ASSOCIATION FOR PSYCHO-LOGICAL SCIENCE, FEELING THAT YOU HAVE A SENSE OF PURPOSE MAY HELP YOU LIVE LONGER, NO MATTER WHAT YOUR AGE!

Purpose with strategy allows you to act tactically. Strategy is the long-term game plan, and tactical steps are the things you can do right now to either get where you're going, or get yourself out of the crap.

So, how do we put this into action?

First, find a purpose. Sometimes you're lucky enough (like me) to have people around you to help you find your purpose. I've had that a lot in my life; people who cared enough to see things I didn't see and put me on a path. But, that's not always the case. So you must start with asking yourself, "What am I passionate about?"

Passion plus purpose equals propulsion. Propulsion to move forward. Propulsion to push past the crap!

After Denny's mentoring revealed my purpose, making Chief in ten years, I was passionate about it. I've had a lot of purposes that I've been passionate about since then, and all have propelled me forward and helped me get past any crap in the way.

And by the way, the path is rarely crap-free, but when you are tied to purpose, you have the energy to keep on going and to keep taking a bite of the crap sandwich.

I was passionate about making my marriage work after my wife's affairs. Actually, in retrospect, I was passionate about being around my kids and for them to grow up to be productive members of society (which has come to fruition). That's what helped me push past. I'm still passionate about being an involved dad (and grandpa!) and I'm passionate about being an amazing husband to my new wife.

I am passionate about my business now and what I do to help people. It was that purpose that pushed me out of the hospital after my ostomy surgery and back to work within ten days. I could have taken more time, felt sorry for myself and let the crap win, but I had a purpose.

What are you passionate about? It could be work related or life related. My parents were passionate about taking us six kids on vacation every year. This was usually a car trip. The thought of a car trip with six kids would, to me, feel like crap; however, for my parents it brought them joy and they thought it was important.

With just one income and six kids, things were always tight financially when we were growing up. A LOT of crap would come their way during the year in between vacations that could have kept my folks from taking a family trip, but they kept on the path and put a little bit away every month so it could happen. Their purpose was their rudder.

For the record, our family trips were before seat belt laws and car seats. The trip wasn't nearly as exhausting for them because we were all in the back of the truck (it had a topper) and they were up in the cab (with no slider window so we could bother them). I often wished on long car trips with my four children that I had a plexiglass barrier, but no such luck.

> **CRAPTASTIC FACT:** THE WISCONSIN–BASED MARSHFIELD CLINIC CONDUCTED A STUDY THAT FOUND "THE ODDS OF DEPRESSION AND TENSION WERE HIGHER AMONG WOMEN WHO TOOK VACATIONS ONLY ONCE IN TWO YEARS COMPARED WITH WOMEN WHO TOOK VACATIONS TWICE OR MORE PER YEAR." IN OTHER WORDS, TAKE VACATIONS! CUT THE STRESS AND TENSION OF EVERYDAY LIFE WITH REGULAR TIME AWAY FROM WORK, EVEN IF IT'S A ROAD TRIP WITH YOUR SIX KIDS.

What is important to you? Find your passion and you'll reveal your purpose. Write it down. Visualize it. See yourself getting there (even if it is just a family vacation to a local campground).

Another way to look for your purpose is to ask yourself what you value. People? Experiences? Money? There is nothing wrong with valuing money or material things, by the way.

I value time with my children. Some days, pushing through the manure with gusto was with the purpose of being able to spend time with them when I got home. Okay, that was when they were younger (and fun) and not so much when they were teenagers.

I value taking care of my team as a leader. With that in mind as a purpose, I could push through the bunk of crappy bosses giving me more crap as long as I kept in mind that it was for the benefit of the whole.

I value being the underdog. I enjoy being the person that can come from the rear and make shit happen regardless of the garbage that is thrown his way.

Having a compelling purpose might seem as simple as just setting a goal. It can be. It can be a larger purpose (i.e. ending world hunger), or as simple as pushing through so you can spend time with your kids. No matter what, have a purpose.

It's important to point out that a person is NOT your purpose. Getting Danny Zuko or Sandy to fall for you, or trying to prove yourself to a person (boss, parent, spouse, etc.) cannot be your purpose. With Denny, I was an investment, not a purpose. I could take his advice or not. He couldn't control that. It was up to me. Helping me with my career was not his purpose and living up to his expectations was not my purpose.

Too many times we throw ourselves into a person, then they go their own way and we get hurt. Don't lose yourself in another person. Love them, invest yourself in them but don't make them your purpose. You'll hate yourself in the morning for it.

When crap comes your way, and it will, remember to take the long-range view. Think strategically and act tactically. Remember what my good old Senior Chief told me, "It's all in 20." Ok, that might not mean much unless you're actually retiring from the military after that amount of time. Go with, "this is just a day." Seriously, just say it. Feel it. When I say it out loud and hear the words from my own mouth, it calms me and allows me to see the possibility of tomorrow.

Focus on possibility. That means do something. Don't be a Ricky. Do one small step. That leads to the next. The stress from piles of crap can immobilize us, yet doing something is always better than doing nothing. Nothing nets nothing. Positive action nets results. Resilient leaders, like you, find a purpose and create a strategy for how they're going to get there. Discover your special purpose and kick some crap ass!

GET PAST THE CRAP!

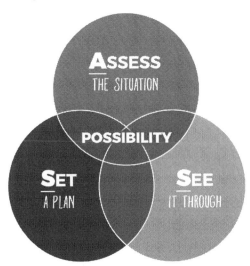

ASSESS YOUR CURRENT SITUATION

Where are you on the Craptometer scale?

LEVEL 1	LEVEL 2	LEVEL 3	LEVEL 4
Everything is **CRAPTASTIC!**	Same Old **CRAP**	**CRAP** is getting **HEAVY**	My Life is **CRAP**

WHAT IS YOUR PURPOSE?

If you are not clear on your purpose, ask yourself:

- What are you passionate about?
- What do you value?

SET A PLAN

1. What has been holding you back or keeping you stuck in the past?
2. What's your long-range view? Where do you see yourself in 1, 5, and 10 years?
3. Who are some resilient leaders you admire that you can emulate?
4. Who can serve as a mentor for you as you work towards your purpose?

SEE IT THROUGH

Write down specific concrete actions:

Today, I will _____
_____.

This week, I will _____
_____.

This month, I will _____
_____.

WRITE DOWN YOUR POSSIBILITY:

CHAPTER 3

GET PAST THE CRAP BY BEING A
POSITIVE THINKER

"Don't cry because it's over, smile because it happened."
–Dr. Seuss

Napoleon Bonaparte once said, "A leader is a dealer in hope." If you expect to lead your team and keep a positive environment, it has to start with you. Again, and always, you have to lead yourself first. The buck might stop here, and it begins here.

Leading isn't all cotton candy and lemon drops. Quite frankly, a lot of times it is a pain in the ass. You not only have your own crap to deal with, you have all the turds of your team too. Couple with that the bilge the boss (or the organization) throws at you, and it's easy to get stressed, depressed and pissed.

When the big baloney sandwich overwhelms us, we can get (what I call) the negative brain. Seriously, that's all we see: negative. We have the negative thoughts like, "This is going to suck!" Which leads to the negative attitude of "We're going to suck." And that might lead to negative behavior. I get it. I've been there. I can't tell you how many times, personally or professionally, my attitude has gotten in my own way in moving forward (and I'm naturally a "glass half-full" kind of person).

I had the negative brain when I was facing divorce. People flat out told me I was morose and they didn't want to be around me. My attitude impacted my energy and the energy of my team.

I had the negative brain after September 11th, 2001. I was serving as the Director of Security for the Naval District. The year prior had been taxing but, because the changes we were going through were purpose driven, I had been able to keep a positive attitude. After 9/11, it was different. Everything was different. My disposition was different. I was responsible for the safety and security of 25,000 people on six different Naval bases in the National Capital region. When I would sit back and look at my job in its totality and my everyday demands, I felt I was way out of my league. I lost my sense of humor. I was not pleasant to be around and, yes, it showed because no one wanted to be around me. Even my kids mutinied (seriously, they mutinied). I got things done but I wasn't as effective because my attitude sucked.

I had the negative brain when I was heading towards bankruptcy. I felt like a failure. One word I had always used to describe myself was responsible. This whole thing went against my core values and it was incongruent with how I saw myself. I was crippled with guilt, despair, and self-loathing. Not a pretty sight.

Having the negative brain isn't special or unique. It happens to all of us. We focus in on the negative because it's how we're wired as humans. Our brains have two different systems for negative and positive stimuli. The amygdala uses approximately two-thirds of its neurons to detect negative experiences, and once the brain starts looking for bad news, it is stored into long-term memory quickly.

A positive experience, on the other hand, has to be held in our awareness for more than twelve seconds in order for it to transfer from short-term to long-term memory. Perhaps this wiring goes back to prehistoric times when we had to focus on the negative because if we didn't, it might eat us.

Further, did you know there are more negative emotional words (62 percent) than positive words (32 percent) in the English dictionary? I know, it freaked me out too.

Thus, if we as leaders are going to be dealers in hope, we need to strive to have more of a positive brain. When we can do that, we can have the same cycle of thought, behavior and attitude and it goes in a much more positive and productive cycle. We can have the positive thoughts of, "Hey, maybe this isn't going to be too bad." Which can lead to the positive attitude of, "Hey, we're going to rock at this!" Which, ultimately, will lead you and the team to the positive behavior of saying, "Hey, we're awesome!"

Your thoughts are a catalyst for self-perpetuating cycles. What you think directly influences how you feel and how you behave. If you think you're a failure, you'll feel like a failure. Then, you'll act like a failure, which reinforces your belief that you *must* be a failure. Once you draw a conclusion about yourself, you're likely to look for evidence that reinforces your belief and discount anything that runs contrary to your belief. It works the same for feeling positive as well. If you think you are a good leader, your brain will look for all the examples when you have shown up as a good leader and give evidence to prove that you are a good leader. So start paying attention to what you think.

> **CRAPTASTIC FACT**
>
> SCIENCE HAS PROVEN THAT YOUR THOUGHTS CHANGE SHAPE OF YOUR BRAIN AND CONSTANT, REGULAR, REPEATED POSITIVE THINKING AND DAILY POSITIVE ACTIONS CAN RE—WIRE YOUR BRAIN, AND MAKE IT STRONGER AND STIMULATE PARTS THAT ALLOW YOU TO ENJOY GREATER SUCCESS!

When I was a young sailor, I ended up working for a particularly mean-hearted man. He wasn't exactly "spawn of Lucifer" mean, but I used to think this guy would sit at home at night thinking of ways to torture and humiliate me. I was his workhorse and he spared me no favors. But, here's the beautiful thing about the military: if you don't like working with someone, it's often short-lived. Either you or the other person is transferring soon, so you usually you can see the light at the end of the tunnel (unlike my father who worked in a steel mill with the same assholes for over forty years).

So, there it was, my transfer date. I could see the light at the end of the tunnel and I was running for that MOFO as fast as I could. I spent my last day going from shop to shop getting my check-out sheet signed off (you had to get it fully completed before you could leave) and this guy was the last person on my list. At the end of the day, I shuffled up to him, and half-mumbled, "Hey, Chief, can you sign my checkout sheet?"

He gave me his normal gruff look and said, "Sure, Chip, but I'm really going to miss you!"

"*WTF!?*" I thought to myself. *You just spent the last year beating me up daily!* But I said, "Hmmm, Chief, why are you going to miss me?"

"Well, Chip, you're more than a mere worker, you're a whole atmosphere…you just make the workplace a little bit better."

I was confused and pleased. Later that night, when I was falling asleep and mulling over the day's events (and when I get my best ideas), I thought, "He's right! I AM AN ATMOSPHERE!" I always tried to make a positive impact and have a joke on the ready to lighten the mood. I had no idea this man had even noticed. Being called an atmosphere is still one of my favorite work compliments ever received.

As leaders, we get to determine what type of atmosphere to create: positive or negative. You really do set the tone.

I see people in two different categories. The first is what I call a

Carrier. A carrier has the negative brain continuously and carries their negativity around like a disease, trying to infect everyone they come into contact with. If a carrier is having a bad day, you can bet they want you to have a bad day too. You know the person: always bitching, complaining, or causing havoc; they are miserable and dead-set on infecting everyone around with the same attitude.

That's not the kind of person we want to choose to be. If you want to take care of yourself first and also create a positive climate, you need to be what I call a Converter. A converter has the positive brain. A converter is more than a spot of sunshine. A converter converts negatives into positives and creates a positive atmosphere. The atmosphere is created because of a condition called emotional contagion which literally means that emotions are contagious. They pass from person to person (this happens both positively and negatively).

You've experienced it. People routinely "catch" each other's feelings when working together in groups. It's not surprising that a leader's atmosphere influences your mood or your team's mood. It's important to know that the atmosphere of leadership significantly influences judgment and business decisions, usually without anyone having a clue what's going on.

Imagine at Joe at work. He always has something positive to say, never joins in the office gossip, is willing to help you out when your computer freezes up, and on and on. When you see Joe, your mood just automatically lightens because you know he is not going to bring any hassles your way. That kind of colleague makes the work environment a better place for everyone. Teams will work harder when they feel they are supported. You, as a leader, start that at the top. If you show up crabby and demanding, how do you think your team is going to respond? It's so simple, but sometimes we don't put the simple things into practice and we let the downward spiral take over.

You know what I'm talking about. Let's say you're in a decent mood. You go home and find your spouse (or significant other) in a bad mood. They yell at you, you then yell at the kid, the kid kicks the dog, the dog bites the cat, and the cat runs away. There you go, cycle of emotions.

You've lived that at work, too, haven't you? Boss is crappy, piles loads of crap on you, and you crap all over everyone around you the entire day. Fortunately, the opposite is also true for the positive and with being a converter.

Let's assume your organization is going through major changes. You don't know how it's going to turn out and your home life is a heaping pile of crap too. You've got the negative brain and you're being a carrier making yourself and everyone around you miserable. You want to be a dealer in hope but it seems hopeless. What do you do? Convert it!

How?

Do something! When I'm in the depths of the negative brain, all I want to do is mope. I know I'm not alone in this. You know the feeling: the crap is waist deep and the only thing that feels good is lying in bed with the blanket over your head (waiting for your mom to come in and tell you that everything is going to be okay).

Motion creates emotion. If you lay around feeling sorry for yourself, the negative brain is going perpetuate itself and you won't ever feel better, you'll feel worse. Science has shown that there is a biochemical link between what you think, what you do, and how you feel. Just the mere act of sitting up straight with your shoulders back, your head up and a smile can improve your mood. So, get out of bed! And yes, even a fake smile works to improve your mood. You gotta start somewhere!

Start each day with PMA. PMA is Positive Mental Attitude. It's a choice. It's intentional. It's Option 3! Every morning, before your feet even touch the ground make a choice to keep the PMA! I always tell myself, this is going to be a F*ING AWESOME DAY! I'll even, sometimes, talk to myself in the third person like,

"LUTZ, YOU MAGNIFICENT BASTARD! YOU'RE GOING TO ROCK THE SHIT OUT OF THIS DAY!"

(You are always much cooler when you refer to yourself in the third person). The choice of PMA is the first step but, as you know, crap happens. And when it does, you need to employ the positive reframe.

The positive reframe is looking at the glass as half full versus half empty. It is finding a silver lining in the situation. It's having an "I can figure this out" perspective instead of one of anger, panic, or blame. It's not always easy but, again, it's a choice.

Two weeks after my ostomy surgery, I was back on the road and back to work. I had a 3-day speaking engagement in Iowa that went off without a hitch. I was still getting used to having a bag stuck to my abdomen, and was always worried that in the middle of a talk it would start leaking. As a side note, with an ostomy bag, it's all about the seal. If you have a good seal, the bag will be fine. If you don't and it bursts, you get a little PTSD (Post Traumatic Seal Disorder) and shit all over you.

> **CRAPTASTIC FACT**
>
> IN THE YEAR 1776, DR. M. PILORE, A FRENCH SURGEON SPECIALIZING IN TREATING BOWEL OBSTRUCTIONS AND OTHER DIGESTIVE TRACT RELATED ILLNESSES, PERFORMED THE FIRST OSTOMY SURGERY.

After Iowa, I had a flight to North Dakota to speak the next day. I was on the second day of the current ostomy bag (they are supposed to last four) so I figured I would be good to go until I had to fly back home. My flight landed, I got to my hotel and quickly fell asleep. At 2am I woke up to a very uncomfortable feeling. My shirt was wet. I jumped out of bed to find out that I was covered in my own crap.

My bag had burst sometime during the night. I honestly felt like crying. I very quickly was slipping into the negative brain. *Why me? Why now? What could I have done to prevent this? Why can't I just get a break with this f'ing bag?*

I jumped in the shower to get cleaned up repeating the whole incident in my head and, yes, wishing my mom would come and tell me everything would be okay. Then it was time for a choice. I could continue to replay this shitty experience in my head, or I could take my own advice and look for the positive. Then I started laughing because: One, I was nearly 50 years old and I just shit the bed. And two, thank God those weren't my sheets!

Of course, I left a big tip for the cleaning crew the next day and that reframe got me through the crap (literally) and through the next day (although I did spend the whole day with PTSD).

Positive reframing does not change the situation, but it can certainly reduce damage and put things into a healthier perspective. Therapists use it frequently as a technique to restructure cognitions. When done skillfully with humor, it can be a wonderful tension de-fuser. Try it and see how a well-placed positive reframe can make a difference in a difficult situation.

One other part of PMA is to concern yourself with what you can control. Let's face it, most of the crap in our lives is out of our hands. We can worry and stress about it, or we can focus on what can be controlled.

Get Past the Crap by Being a Positive Thinker

I travel a lot with my job. I used to spend a lot time worrying about making connecting flights and the "what ifs" of what would happen if I didn't. It was a bunch of unnecessary stress weighing on me every time I travelled and usually anger, angst, and negative thoughts would follow. Now, I am pretty amazing at many things, but I can't control the comings and goings of the air traffic that I was so reliant on. So, I bought the Scrabble app for my iPhone because I can control what letters make what words. When I found myself being pulled into the negative spiral when travelling, I would play Scrabble instead and realize that I had control of that circumstance (I even got to make the word "poopy" one time).

We all always have a choice. On D-Day, June 6th, 1944, General Dwight D. Eisenhower was in charge of the largest amphibious assault ever contemplated. All of the forces were out to sea waiting for the "go" from Ike, and he was waiting for the weather to clear so they could proceed. If they didn't go that day, they'd have to come back in and it would be six months before they would be able to attempt the invasion again (and by then it would be too late). Finally, when the weather cleared, he gave the go ahead. Then, according to his biography, he said, "I hope to hell I know what I'm doing" and went to lay down. He knew at that point it was out of his hands. General Eisenhower focused on what he could control, a great lesson for all of us.

Focus on what you can control or what you can't control will control you.

> **CRAPTASTIC FACT**
>
> A RECENT STUDY SUGGESTS A STRONG CORRELATION BETWEEN WEARING CERTAIN CLOTHES AND EMOTIONAL STATES. FOR EXAMPLE, WOMEN WHO ARE DEPRESSED OR SAD ARE MORE LIKELY TO WEAR BAGGY TOPS, SWEATSHIRTS, OR JEANS. WOMEN WHO HAD MORE POSITIVE EMOTIONS WERE MORE LIKELY TO WEAR A FAVORITE DRESS OR JEWELRY. "LOOK GOOD, FEEL GOOD" IS REAL SO START YOUR PMA BY DRESSING FOR SUCCESS IN CLOTHES THAT MAKE YOU FEEL COMFORTABLE AND CONFIDENT.

Another tactic positive thinkers employ is to surround yourself with other converters. This is the best way for me to keep a positive attitude. Let's face it, we need people. Even if you're an introvert, you still need people. Choose to be around people that build you up, not those who tear you down. Me? I'm going to surround myself with the people that make me laugh.

When you do have to be around the negative folks of the world, remember a few things in dealing with them. You can't control other people but you can control how you interact with them.

I have four brothers. I love them all the time but that doesn't mean I like them all the time. One of my brothers and I are on completely different spectrums on a variety of issues. You name it, we see it differently. This used to result in an argument any time we would get together. It was exhausting and was damaging our relationship (and I would have a seriously negative brain after each time we'd get together). I was tired of it so I set up the ROE (Rules of Engagement) prior to his visits. I would tell him ahead of time the subjects that were "off limits" for us to talk about and give him the same respect. We both stayed away from those subjects and, amazingly, our relationship and our attitudes towards each other improved.

You can do the same thing with the people in your own life - personal or professional.

When dealing with carriers, remember that drama can't exist in a vacuum. Carriers want to suck you into their crap. Drama loves drama. What's important to remember is what was mentioned before: emotions are contagious so you need to have a strategy on how to keep their drama-laden crap from becoming yours.

Very much like with strategy and distractions, all you need to do is ask yourself, "Is this drama something that I care about?" If it is, engage, but keep your emotional distance. If not, walk away. Most of the things I care directly about are very Chip-centric (i.e. wife, kids, career, grandchildren). My mental wellbeing and keeping a positive outlook is much too important to get sucked into OPD (Other People's Drama). Negative drama can't exist on its own. It needs company. Don't take the bait.

You may or may not be a converter by nature. Even if you are, there are times when the sewage is so thick that it seems impossible to dig yourself out. Yet you know that's not true. You always have the choice to take a big bite out of the old crap sandwich. Option 3 is always the road to choose. Every day I make a choice to have PMA and do the things necessary to keep my own attitude in check. You do the same! You absolutely can be a dealer in hope. It always starts with yourself first. As a resilient leader, you get to set the atmosphere. And you also get to say goodbye to the negative brain. There's no time like the present so start today!

GET PAST THE CRAP!

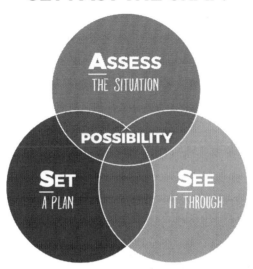

ASSESS YOUR CURRENT SITUATION

Where are you on the Craptometer scale?

ARE YOU A POSITIVE THINKER?

- Are you a Carrier or a Converter as a leader?
- Do you even pay attention to your attitude? Start now!

SET A PLAN

1. What helps you start the day with PMA?
2. What is a way you can reframe the crap that you're facing?
3. Who are the people that build you up and are fun to be around?
4. Notice what drama others sucked you into lately and make efforts to stay out of it.

SEE IT THROUGH

Write down specific concrete actions:

Today, I will _____.

This week, I will _____.

This month, I will _____.

WRITE DOWN YOUR POSSIBILITY:

_____
_____
_____
_____
_____
_____
_____
_____
_____
_____
_____
_____
_____
_____
_____
_____
_____
_____
_____
_____
_____

CHAPTER 4

GET PAST THE CRAP BY
PAYING ATTENTION

"I shall look at you out of the corner of my eye, and you will say nothing. Words are the source of misunderstandings."
–Antoine de Saint-Exupéry

In any conversation, there is what's said, what's heard, and what's meant; rarely are they the same thing. That's the kind of ca-ca that can stress you out, weigh you down, and cause huge problems in all aspects of your life.

THAT'S WHY RESILIENT LEADERS MUST PAY ATTENTION!

You need to pay attention to what's being said, what's not being said, who's not saying what, who is saying too much, how it's being said, who is saying what to who, if no one is telling you anything, and if people are "bumping uglies" in the break room (just threw that one in to see if you were paying attention) (that, by the way, was a term my dad used for people having sex… just to clarify).

Surveys, studies, and common sense will tell you that communication issues are the number one source of stress within the workplace. Issues range from not feeling heard, miscommunication, to angry tones being used. What's going in your environment and what can you do about it? Are you even aware of what your team thinks about workplace communication?

When we don't pay attention, we get a lot of what I call "Taco Body" moments and that can cause even more problems to come our way. Let me explain. My youngest son, Ben, loves music. When he was only two years old, he had all the words to "Love Machine" memorized. He would stand up in his high chair and do his little diaper dance along to it (it was really cute, you had to be there). When Ben was about nine, the 80's song "Funky Town" by a group called Lips Incorporated came on the radio. Do you remember that one? It's a great song that spans most generations.

Anyway, one day as Ben was hanging out in the living room building spaceships with his Legos, that song was blaring in the background and, of course, Ben was singing along at the top of his lungs. When they started singing, "talk about it, talk about it, talk about it, talk about it…" Ben, belted out "Taco body, taco body, taco body, taco body…"

Confused, I looked at him and asked, "Taco body?"

Without missing a beat (and with confident sincerity), he nodded and replied, "Yeah, Taco Body!"

"TACO BODY!?" WHAT THE HELL? Then I realized this is what happens to us every day, isn't it? We're singing "talk about it" and everybody out there is hearing "Taco Body" (and vice versa).

We've all sat through the communication classes. We know the basics of good communication, but everyone is still hearing taco body!

On a side note, after I shared this story in my keynote talks, I've been informed of all kinds of misheard lyrics. Credence Clearwater Revival's "There's a Bad Moon On The Rise" was "There's a bathroom on the right." Elton John sings, "Hold me closer, Tony Danza," or I guess he really said, "Tiny Dancer." Does anyone really know for sure? Anyway, in life at home and at work, taco body moments aren't funny when miscommunication happens.

TODAY, THERE ARE OVER 6,000 LANGUAGES SPOKEN IN THE WORLD. IN PAPUA NEW GUINEA ALONE, OVER 800 LANGUAGES ARE SPOKEN.

I had a coaching client share his frustrations with me about how he never found out something was an issue until after the fact. Carl had weekly meetings with his whole team on the strategy for the week and then the next week, when they'd review what was supposed to be done, it either wasn't done or wasn't done the right way. It was stressful for Carl and his team. When we pared down to the root causes, it simply was too many taco body moments. Both sides listened to what they thought they heard and never went back to clarify if those were really the words to the song.

If you want to have crap-resistant communication, you have to pay attention to everything. Please note I did not say crap-free communication. That never happens BUT you can have crap-resistant if you work at it. I had an equation that I used for over twenty years in the Navy (and still use today) so that I can make sure I am hearing what is being said. I keep it posted it on my computer so I can be present in the conversation. Here it is:

$$Q2L + S2S + S2A = GR8\ COMMS$$

Simply translated:

Q2L *[Quick To Listen]*
+ S2S *[Slow To Speak]*
+ S2A *[Slow To Anger]*
= GR8 COMMS *[Great Communication]*

I'd love to take credit for this (I will with the equation), but the complete thought comes from the New Testament of the Bible in the book of James. Yes, I go to church and even teach Sunday School (shocking given my Sailor's Mouth?). Let's break down how the equation can help you pay attention.

Being quick to listen means that if we're listening, we're not talking. So, yes, the first step in effective listening is to shut up!

A study of over 8,000 people employed in businesses, hospitals, universities, the military and government agencies found that virtually all the respondents believed that they communicate as effectively or more effectively than their co-workers. However, research shows that the average person listens at only about 25% efficiency. While most people agree that listening effectively is a very important skill, most people don't feel a strong need to improve their own skill level.

Before my dad passed away, every day at 6:50am, he would head out to meet with his posse for a donut and coffee. His gang consisted of guys he's known for decades and, like him, were retired. Whenever I would go home to visit, I would join him in this daily ritual. In addition to cutting the median age in half (just by being there), I also got to watch these men (who knew each other all too well) interact.

This group of guys mirrored what happens to us every day with listening (or lack of) that can cause huge mounds of buffalo chips to come our way. All these men used hearing aids, but they either didn't have them turned up or weren't wearing them at all. Leaders have hearing aids as well and, yes, sometimes we don't have them turned up or don't wear them. Our hearing aids are that of retention, absenteeism, productivity, and the overall morale of the team. When we tune those things out, we lose focus of what leading is really all about: people!

We can tune in by paying attention to all those things, but by also by tuning into what our people are talking about in the hallways. Get out and about and listen to what's going on. You'll learn a lot by turning up the hearing aid!

Second, the same conversation among my dad and his pals took place nearly every day. They said the same stuff on Thursday that they had on Tuesday. They were talking just to talk. Ever know a leader like that? Leaders sometimes run a script too. We say what we think a leader needs to say rather than what we, as people, should say. Scripts are great for actors but not for leaders.

So stop talking and do more listening. Listening is a full body event. It's not enough to just listen to what's being said, we have to listen for feelings and with empathy. The other thing I noticed sitting at this table with my dad: everyone talked but no one listened.

> YOUR EARS WORK A LITTLE FASTER THAN YOUR MOUTH. THE AVERAGE NUMBER OF WORDS YOU'RE ABLE TO LISTEN TO PER MINUTE IS AROUND 450. SOME PEOPLE ARE CHATTIER THAN OTHERS BUT ON AVERAGE, THE TYPICAL PERSON UTTERS ANYWHERE FROM 125 TO 175 WORDS PER MINUTE.

I've been in meetings with all talkers and no listeners, and believe that this is how most of society operates (as it did with the coaching client I mentioned earlier). Everyone wants to be heard, but no one wants to do the hearing. I'm as guilty as everyone else in this regard. I have to remind myself that less is more in communicating. In that, less talking means more listening. Take a break, take notes or take yourself out of the conversation. In the end, everyone wants to be heard and more listening leads to less crap.

Another concept I want to mention about listening is that you have to kill your monkeys.

Buddhists have a term called monkey mind. Buddha described the human mind as being filled with drunken monkeys that are jumping around, screeching, chattering, and carrying on endlessly. We all have *monkey minds,* Buddha said, with dozens of monkeys all clamoring for attention. These monkeys are the barriers that keep us from effectively listening. You might have the monkey of not liking the person you're talking to. You have the email monkey that is beckoning you back to your computer. You have the smartphone monkey that lures you into Facebook for the very important information of seeing what people are eating. I have some monkeys that are just flinging poo on other monkeys and having fun. Be aware of your monkeys and kill them if you want to be truly paying attention.

Let me explain further. After a presentation recently, a woman, Nancy, came up to speak to me about her monkey (that didn't really sound right…). Her busiest day of the week was Wednesday. Nancy told me that it was her power meeting day and that, normally, all meetings went back to back. At the end of the day she'd get back to her office to a full email inbox and a line of people waiting to see her (all of which needed some kind of decision to be made on something). Nancy said that she tried to pay attention to what was being said in the conversation but all she could think about were all of the emails she had to get through before she could go home. Yes, the dreaded email monkey. The only way she could kill that monkey was to physically separate herself from her office and meet with people in the conference room. Drastic? Not if it killed the monkey so she could pay attention.

What are your monkeys? How are you going to kill them?

Being slow to speak is sometimes just as hard as listening, but obviously works in tandem. If you're not running the script, you are paying attention. If you've killed your monkeys, you're paying attention. If you have your hearing aids on, you're paying attention. If you're slow to speak, you must be paying attention.

When you do have to say something, you also must pay attention to what you're going to say and how you're going to say it. Have you ever had that ill-spoken word and then a milli-second later, your stomach lurches as you think, *Why in the hell did I just say that?!* Or you go to say something and it comes out wrong? The tone was wrong or the wording was wrong or the timing was wrong?

It's happened to me on more than one occasion and can cause a lot of crap. That's why I'm a proponent of having the difficult conversation before the conversation. This is different from running a script. A script requires no thought. You are just going through the motions and saying what you think the situation requires. Having the conversation before the conversation requires quite a bit of pre-thought and of thinking about the other person and possible scenarios. This is something I've done for years that has drastically reduced the crap in my life.

HOW DO YOU GO ABOUT HAVING IT BEFORE YOU HAVE IT?

First, think about worst case. What's the worst way the conversation can go? What will I say? What are my major points and how will I respond when things start going bad? How am I going to keep my cool and not make things worse? (I don't have anger issues but I do have triggers...which I'll cover in a few minutes).

Second, think about best case. If the stars align and manna starts falling from heaven, how will I respond? What words will I use to express my appreciation? How do I lead the conversation to best case (i.e. showing the value of my side).

Last, think about how to close. Best case or worst case, I want to make sure I leave the conversation on an upbeat note. I also want to make sure I don't forget anything so I'll make a mental note of the follow up on things that need to be done. Choose the time, the place and your words carefully. A proactive conversation will monumentally decrease the amount of cowpies you're going to have to deal with...unless you hold onto the issue too long and then tempers flare.

When I'm angry, my ears are off and I'm not hearing anything. When the person I'm talking to is angry, the same applies. There is no larger heap of crap that mires us down more than anger. And, let's face it, we live in an angry world. It's all over the place. Turn on the TV, people are angry. Open up Facebook, people are angry. Talk to your spouse after not doing what she asked, she is angry. To quote Rodney King,"Why can't we all just get along?" We can if we're paying attention. Pay attention to your own triggers and also try to see things from the other person's point of view.

> **CRAPTASTIC FACT**
>
> ANGER IS MORE THAN JUST AN EMOTION, IT ACTUALLY HAS PHYSIOLOGICAL EFFECTS THAT OCCUR ALONGSIDE OF IT. THESE RANGE FROM RACING HEARTBEATS, SWEATING, AND INCREASE IN BLOOD PRESSURE.

Before I retired from the Navy, I started teaching at night. I loved it and it was the catalyst for what I do now as a professional speaker. My first semester was fantastic. I connected fabulously with the class, everyone was respectful, and we all learned something along the way (myself included). My second semester, however, things went a little sideways because I wasn't aware of my own anger triggers.

The first week of that semester, I started out as usual: high energy and getting to know the class. Two rows back, right in the middle was a young man (about 22 years old) that was a Chatty Cathy (my apologies to any Cathy's out there that are not chatty and are offended by the term). This guy would talk over me to his neighbors, make jokes and be a little disruptive. Now, Leadership 101 would tell you that if there is an issue with someone, you address it early. I, however, did not do this. Although I knew what I should do, this was a new environment and I did not apply the known. I did my best to ignore him.

Second week, it was the same story. Third week, the same. Again, I did nothing but hold on to my frustration until the fourth week. Week 4 it was the same case but, in addition to being disruptive, the talkative obnoxious fellow started texting and smirking at me.

I lost it. What I meant to say to this student, in a kind and gentle tone: "Hey, if you don't want to be here, please go ahead and leave."

What actually came out of my mouth, in a very stern, loud, militant manner :"IF YOU DON'T WANT TO BE HERE, THERE'S THE F'ING DOOR!"

He left immediately, I ended class early, and the subject line on the email I sent my Dean was, "You may have to fire me."

From experience, I know that disrespect is a trigger for me and can cause me to say and do things that cause a ton of crap for myself. In knowing this, I try to find work-arounds so that my anger doesn't get the better of me. In this example, I waited too long. The situation needed to be addressed from the beginning. He was a disruption for the entire class. Many of the students came up to thank me later, but we all knew I could have handled the situation better. And I didn't get fired, by the way.

If a situation is a trigger, stay away. If a person is a trigger, stay away (or set up the rules of engagement early as I stated earlier). KNOW YOUR TRIGGERS!

When something is important, address it early on. And remember to have the conversation before the conversation so you've thought it out and are prepared. Don't ignore a storm that is brewing and don't hold onto your anger and frustration.

We can get really angry when we're running down one path and then find out later that we've be doing it wrong, or that things are different than we expected. To circumvent these kind of situations, look at it from the other person's point of view and think of clarifying questions you can ask.

That was the case when renovating my first house. There wasn't an inch of that house that I hadn't torn apart, rebuilt, repainted, or retouched. I am not the epitome of a handyman, but I was pretty proud that I had done all the work myself. Everything was finally completed with the exception of the entry hallway and my plan was to paint it when I got home that night (after I poured myself a vodka tonic, of course).

Imagine my surprise when I walked in the front door that evening, prepared to get messy with paint, and I see that the hallway was done. Had elves suddenly showed up at our house? And if so, where had they been for all the other projects? This is the conversation with my ex-wife that followed (*disclaimer: this conversation wasn't the cause of our divorce*):

Me: Who painted the hallway?

Her: I did.

Me: When did you learn how to paint?

Her: I've always known how to paint.

Me: If you've always known how to paint, why is it that, for 15 years, I've painted every wall, board, tile or trim?

Her: You never asked.

NEVER ASKED!? Well, holy crap! That hit me like a ton of bricks. Although a little infuriating, she was right. I never did ask. I knew that I knew how to paint, and that I was a little particular, so I just did it. I never once asked her if she wanted to paint.

What have you never thought to ask?

Asking questions can reduce the crap that comes from anger. Further, it helps us understand where the other person is coming from and allows us to pay closer attention to their needs.

Resilient leaders pay attention, in personal communication and at the workplace. You need to start paying close attention to your own communication style. If your team is not operating like you want, it could be you all are experiencing some taco body moments. Listening skills are not something to merely talk about at a communication workshop. Start paying attention to how you pay attention. Notice how you can improve. The leader sets the atmosphere, and communication is part of that atmosphere. Use the communication equation I created and then see how much less crap you have to deal with it. You're welcome.

GET PAST THE CRAP!

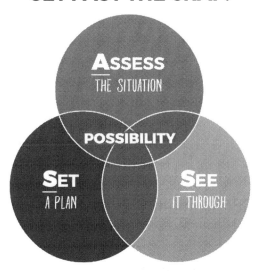

ASSESS YOUR CURRENT SITUATION

Where are you on the Craptometer scale?

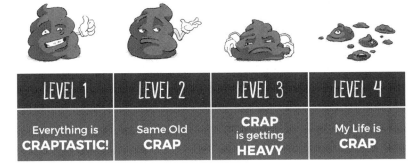

LEVEL 1	LEVEL 2	LEVEL 3	LEVEL 4
Everything is **CRAPTASTIC!**	Same Old **CRAP**	**CRAP** is getting **HEAVY**	My Life is **CRAP**

ARE YOU TRULY PAYING ATTENTION?

- Are you having too many Taco Body moments?
- Do you show up with your "hearing aids" turned on and up?

SET A PLAN

1. Notice when you are in the moment and truly paying attention versus just running the script.
2. What barriers keep you from listening? Your team? Kill those monkeys.
3. What triggers your anger?
4. Implement the Q2L + S2S + S2S = GR8 COMMS formula or create one of your own.

SEE IT THROUGH

Write down specific concrete actions:

Today, I will _____
_____.

This week, I will _____
_____.

This month, I will _____
_____.

WRITE DOWN YOUR POSSIBILITY:

CHAPTER 5

GET PAST THE CRAP BY BEING
PLIABLE

"The measure of intelligence is the ability to change."
—Albert Einstein

Blessed are the flexible for they shall not be bent out of shape. We live in a world of constant change. Change that can seem like it is hurling at us like a F-5 tornado, destroying everything in its path. Even if it's not that dramatic, change can mire us in a humongous, thick, stinky mound of applesauce. What? Applesauce? Yep, I just read applesauce is a synonym for crap. Actually, my beloved mother-in-law (Dixie) uses applesauce as a curse word. (My charming wife obviously didn't learn to curse from her.)

Anyway, we can get bent out of shape when things don't go as we expect, or our routine is broken, or a fresh pile of crap gets stuck to our unsuspecting shoe. That's why resilient leaders choose to be pliable. Yes, it is a choice. See a theme here?

Being pliable is akin to being like a willow tree. Think about the willow tree for a minute. Think about any tree and ride the metaphor with me. We have our roots firmly planted in who we are and where we come from. We have our trunk, thick and solid in the things that we value. It's our branches that make the difference. An oak tree whose branches are brittle and will break when the winds of shit come. The willow is flexible, bending, and able to blow/go with the flow. When we choose to be pliable like a willow, we don't get as stressed, we bounce back and get past our crap so much quicker and easier.

But, let's face it. That's not how we all are built. We human beings love our routines. We feel comfortable with the status quo. Sure, we might venture away from what we know once in a while, but we always venture back to the familiar. Change is not always something we choose to see in a positive manner.

Now don't get me wrong. Some routines are good, like the routines you have that push you towards success or the routines that help you streamline time. The advice I gave my daughter before her first deployment to South Korea was "get into a routine fast…it will help time go faster." I get that. I love those routines. I get up by 5am every day, have a routine that I follow to ensure that I hit my goals. Goals are good. Routines can be good.

However, if I get too entrenched in a routine, any poo flung my way can stress me out and pull me down. If I am too stringent with my routine, I can become a real jerk to be around. I used to be so set in my routines that you'd have to ask me at least a day ahead if you wanted me to make any kind of change in my schedule for the next day. My plans were my plans and I liked my ducks in a row the way that I lined them up. If you asked me the day of to change my schedule, I'd push as hard back as I could to stay within the confines of my world. That was until I started practicing pliability.

Practicing pliability is about pushing yourself out of your routine so you're like the willow and not the oak. The more you're able to flex up top, the less crap is going to break your branches. Practicing pliability comes in two waves, changing our thoughts and changing our actions.

Changing our thoughts takes some practice. We are who we are, or so we tell ourselves. We see things a certain way, based on our roots and our routes. Our roots are where we come from and how we see ourselves within our world. For instance, I'm from the Midwest. I come from a large family and am the youngest of six children. My dad was a blue-collar worker who spent his whole life working in a steel mill to provide for his family and instilled a strong work ethic and sense of family in all of us kids. Those are my roots. (And I like donuts…really anything sweet).

My routes are the intersections that life has taken me: I joined the Navy right out of high school, worked hard and spent twenty-two years serving my country. I've worked with some amazing people who took the time to teach me great lessons. I also worked with a few major league assholes who taught me things, too (mostly through their shitty example). I am twice divorced (same woman), three times married, have four children and two grandchildren. Those are just a few of my routes. (And did I mention…I like donuts).

Our roots and our routes, coupled with our routines can make us rigid. Too rigid to embrace the changes needed at work. Too rigid to deal with the changes needed at home. Too rigid to live outside our comfort zone, experience life and new people. Thankfully we can get past that with strategies for looking at things differently versus just our own view.

THE ABILITY OF THE BRAIN TO MODIFY ITSELF AND ADAPT TO CHALLENGES OF THE ENVIRONMENT IS REFERRED TO AS PLASTICITY.

One way to look at things differently and change your thoughts is to harness the power of the word "Not." Think about that tiny word for a minute; it's pretty powerful. Any time you put it in or out of a statement or phrase, it changes the entire meaning. For instance, YOU are awesome! YOU are NOT awesome. Huge difference, eh?

Henry VIII put the King in Kingship. All the kings before him, in my opinion, were just mere warlords. Henry, on the other hand, with his giant ego and belief that God personally anointed him to rule, brought new meaning in what it meant to be King of England. Seriously, this was a guy who had his own personal butt wiper entitled, "The Groom of the Stool." Which, by the way, was one of the best jobs to have in his court because you were closest to the king (albeit a crappy job (pun intended)).

Henry was not originally meant to be King. He was the second born to Henry VII but with his brother's untimely death, Henry was put at the forefront to rule. After the death of his father in 1509, Henry (at the tender age of 17), assumed the role of King, dutifully married his brother's wife, Catherine of Aragon, and set on a nearly 40-year path that changed the trajectory for the country and all its inhabitants.

With all his ego-induced faults, I think that Henry has gotten a bad rap over the years. Sure, he was a lecher. Yes, he overindulged in sins of the flesh. True, he absolutely was absolute in his divine rightness to rule. Even with his gluttonous faults, he was a trailblazer and a master at instituting change. How did he do this? Henry was able to harness the power of "NOT!"

There is a glut of things that we, as leaders, don't want to emulate from old King Henry. But, knowing how to harness the power of "not" is something to follow.

Henry, after being married to Catherine of Aragon for 15+ years, fell prey to the wants of his heart and fell in love with a lovely young woman named Anne Boleyn. Anne's dark hair, fair skin, and intellect captivated the King in such a way that he knew, above all things, he wanted her. He wanted Anne to be his queen and provide him with a long awaited male heir. In this, he was clear.

Henry's want for Anne to be his Queen posed a bit of a problem. Mainly, because he was legally married to Catherine. In order for him to fulfill his dream he would need an annulment from the Pope. At that time, the only person who had a "step up" on royalty was the Pope.

Henry made his case to the Pope. He sent letters, arguments and envoys to Rome, repeatedly, to get his marriage to Catherine annulled on the basis that since he married his brother's wife, it was an abomination to God and, therefore, not legal. He even tried to convince Catherine to acquiesce and go live in a nunnery. And, even though she knew he was a bit of an ass, she liked being Queen and basically told him to bug off.

No matter what Henry tried to do, it didn't work. The Pope said "No" and that was an absolute because he was the head of the Church.

Henry, although frustrated, was not dismayed. Henry harnessed the power of "NOT" and thought, "Hmmm.... what if the Pope was **NOT** the head of the Church? What if I was head of the church? Then I, Henry, could do anything I wanted!"

That's when it happened: Henry created a new church, made himself the head of it, got rid of his wife, and married Anne Boleyn. That's the short version.

What do you currently view as an absolute that you can insert a "Not"? Challenge your thinking. Look past the roots, routes, and routine. Look at things differently and get past the crap that is confining your cranium!

Harnessing "not" opens up possibility and pliability. Because, when we don't know something, EVERYTHING is a possibility!

Another way to challenge your thoughts to be more pliable is to ask "WHY?" Why is it like it is? Why can't I do it differently? Why is this guy such an asshole? Why am I being such an asshole?

I love when I get the opportunity to babysit my granddaughter. Watching her explore and learn new things is as exciting for me as it is for her. Everything, right now, is "What's that!?" Having been through this stage with my own four children, I know that the next stage is the "Why?" stage. Every new thing will be countered with a question of "Why?" so that she'll be able to understand it and fit it into her schema of the world.

Asking "Why?" is critical. That question helps us get to the root, figure out if it makes sense and then, if it doesn't make sense, figure out how it can. But somewhere down the line as adults, we quit asking the question and just accept things as they are. (I think that's where the phrase "it is what it is" spurs from).

Why do we quit asking why? We're conditioned to quit asking, aren't we? Not overtly, but through the deflecting of the answer by those who don't know how to answer.

When I was twelve, I loved watching the police drama *Hill Street Blues*. This was way back before Google so when they used a word that I had never heard before, I would simply ask my mom. One such evening this occurred. The word? Orgasm.

Mom was no stranger to random questions from her six kids. Mostly from me. This time, however, I caught her off guard. She told me to look it up in the dictionary. I grabbed our tattered dictionary and went to work looking it up. Unfortunately, not knowing the spelling of the word caused a little mix up and the word I found was Organism.

"WHAT!?" I thought. Knowing that this word didn't make any sense in the context it was used in the show, I went back to my mother, dictionary in hand, and showed her the word.

"This doesn't make any sense," I said.

"It's the wrong word," she replied. "This is the right word." She pointed to the definition of orgasm. After reading it and still being confused, I asked, "Have you ever had an orgasm?"

Not missing a beat my mom replied with, "Would you like a cookie?" and deflected the entire conversation to the cravings of a hungry fat kid.

A RECENT STUDY FOUND THAT 48% OF REGULAR HEADACHE SUFFERERS HAD THEIR PAIN CURED BY ORGASM. NOT ONLY THAT, IT ACTUALLY WORKED FASTER THAN PAINKILLERS.

All through life, we are conditioned to accept and not ask why. It's time for that to change. Ask and then ask again. When you keep asking, you keep learning. As you keep learning, you're practicing pliability and you'll bounce back faster.

Dr. Madalyn Blair wrote in *Psychology Today*: "Curiosity is a fundamental trait of the resilient leaders I work with and study. A question about growing deep knowledge tells me that the individual is aware of themselves. When you are aware of yourself, you are always in a place of learning about yourself. And as you learn about yourself, you become more and more acquainted with what is important to you, what drives you, your limitations, and what dreams you have. It's this kind of thinking that leads to a person discovering their purpose. Purpose breeds confidence, and confidence provides the energy to be resilient by acting on ideas you dream up to overcome the block or challenge or change that one is being called upon to be resilient about."

Now that is a paragraph to read more than once. Curiosity is good. Self-awareness is too. Learning about yourself leads to purpose. Purpose (our first way to help you get past your crap) breeds confidence and helps you be more resilient. A lot of amazing stuff can happen when you change your thoughts.

Changing our actions is just as important as changing our thoughts. It doesn't have to be a huge change and it can be easy if we're already challenging our thoughts.

Start with finding ways to say YES. Saying yes can be scary and does entail an element of risk, but as the saying goes, without risk there is no reward. Think of anything great you've ever accomplished in your life. It was when you said no to the quo and yes to the mess! You stepped outside of your comfort zone and did something different. Think about your own life. Use my partial list here to get your ideas flowing.

- Saying "Yes" brought me into the Navy.

- Saying "Yes" gave me challenging jobs that no one else wanted.

- Saying "Yes" has pushed me outside my comfort zone.

- Saying "Yes" had led me to a great speaking/coaching/consulting career.

- Saying "Yes" has provided me a loving new wife.

- Saying "Yes" has taught me everything I know.

- Even when so-called "better judgement" pushed me to say "No" I still said "Yes!"

Why? Because I look at each situation one of two ways:

1. It's going to work out how I envision.
2. It's not going to work out how I envision.

IT'S THAT SIMPLE.

Either way, I'm going to learn something AND I'm calibrating my brain for pliability. Pliability eliminates a lot of the crap before it even starts to smell. Pliability also makes life a lot more fun.

A few years ago, I was in Florida speaking for an association and had the opportunity to visit some good friends. Joe and Fran are like surrogate parents to me so whenever I'm in town, it's like the prodigal son has returned: they kill the fatted calf and we have a feast. As we ate and drank (the wine was flowing very fast from a cardboard box), Joe shared a fantastic story about how just the week before he had gone skydiving.

I don't like heights. That's why I joined the Navy (I'm a good swimmer and I've never seen any reason to jump out of a perfectly good airplane). But, as stated, the wine had been flowing and I said, "We should go do that."

Granted, it was an alcohol-induced YES, but the next day found me 14,000 feet in the air with a man strapped to my back (it was a tandem jump). The jump was exhilarating and changed my perspectives on heights (it even changed my perspective on being tethered to another man because if I could have had him closer, I would have).

Saying YES brought me to another great experience so what keeps us from saying yes, taking a risk and embracing change? Fear.

Fear is a mother f'er. We fear seeing things differently, doing something differently or meeting someone different. Frankly, that all is just a load of hooey nonsense crap.

You can start small and it has big effects on your pliability. You don't have to jump out of a plane to face fear or change up your routine. For example, if you take the same way to work all the time, say yes to trying a new way. If you eat the same food all the time, say yes to trying a new dish. If you're a right-handed washer in the shower, switch to your left hand (you might spend that day being stinky). Every small change in routine helps you when the big waves of change/crap come. (Note: I will not say yes to my adult children moving back in with me. I like my routine of walking around in my underwear too much).

An even easier way of changing up our actions is to change where our actions take place. Shift up the environment. Include the people you're around and find someone to push you past your norm.

My job as a speaker/consultant puts me in new cities and new environments all the time. Even so, I mainly stick with my norm of staying in my hotel room in the evenings. I have a comfortable bed, free wifi, and Netflix to catch up on. This, however, drives my wife crazy. When Gwen doesn't travel with me, she calls and asks what I'm doing. When I refer to my routine, she replies, "I don't understand why you'd be in a new town and not see anything!"

When she does travel with me, it's a completely different story. She drags me out to see the great big world, and while I'm working, she certainly doesn't stay in the hotel watching old movies. One example was San Francisco. I was speaking and emceeing all day, so Gwen hit the town. At the end of the day when I finally found her, she shared her adventures of exploring the whole town and all the sights, touring it with strangers who were now her friends, and all the new things she experienced. She was on Cloud 9. Gwen wasn't going to wait for me to try something new, she got past that crap with ease. Whether traveling or at home, my wife continually pushes me outside of my routine to do something different all the time.

Not too long ago, Gwen informed me that two people from Finland were stopping by our house when they came to the United States. When I asked her how she met them, she said, "Oh, that's the friend I met on Instagram."

I replied, "How do you know they're not axe murderers?" (I watch too much crime TV). When they did visit, it was awesome. We got to experience new people and a new culture (they cooked a traditional Finnish meal for us). When talking with the husband, I was amused to see how just alike we were. He had asked his wife the same thing when she said they were coming to our house, "How do you know they're not axe murderers?"

The point is that sometimes we need people that stretch us outside our comfort zone. Get a friend that does that for you. If you can't find someone and you need a push, ask yourself

WWGD? (What Would Gwen Do?) And do that. She's always in for something new and explores new situations with a childlike innocence. What's nice about a friend like that is not only do they make you do different things, they usually see things much differently than you which also helps change your thoughts. Who knows, maybe you'll be inviting strangers from Finland to come stay at your house.

The key to getting past your crap is not about changing who you are, it's all about becoming more pliable. Become more open to new thoughts and new actions. Resilient leaders maintain their core values but also realize how roots and routes have shaped them. Understanding that you can be grounded and also move like the willow tree that bends with the winds of change allows you to have a much happier life. If you can handle stress and change with less internal and external upset, imagine how different your life will be. Imagine how much better your team will feel and operate. It's time to flex and allow that possibility to be your reality.

GET PAST THE CRAP!

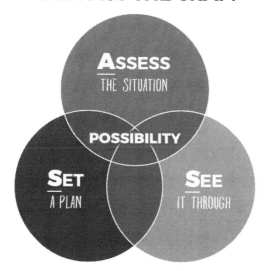

ASSESS YOUR CURRENT SITUATION

Where are you on the Craptometer scale?

LEVEL 1	LEVEL 2	LEVEL 3	LEVEL 4
Everything is **CRAPTASTIC!**	Same Old **CRAP**	**CRAP** is getting **HEAVY**	My Life is **CRAP**

ARE YOU PLIABLE?

- What changes are stressing you out the most?
- What routines are holding you back?

SET A PLAN

1. Ask yourself "WHY" things are the way they are (5 times to get to root).
2. What is one thing that you can harness the power of "NOT" to get a new perspective?
3. What is something you can say "YES" to?
4. Who is that friend that continually pushes you out of your comfort zone (WWGD)?

SEE IT THROUGH

Write down specific concrete actions:

Today, I will _____
_____.

This week, I will _____
_____.

This month, I will _____
_____.

WRITE DOWN YOUR POSSIBILITY:

CHAPTER 6

GET PAST THE CRAP WITH
PRACTICE

*"Practice isn't the thing you do once you're good.
It's the thing you do that makes you good."*
—Malcolm Gladwell

You can't run a marathon without putting band aids on your nipples. Why? Chafing. You need something to protect you from the pain. And, in the marathon of life, the crap we deal with does the same. It rubs us raw and sometimes we reach for the wrong band aids.

When we're ripped apart by the crap that is being flung at us, we reach for something that will fill the gaping hole the crap has created and, instead of filling it with things that bring happiness, we fill it with MORE crap! We go shopping. We buy a new car. We flirt with the person at the checkout stand (ok, that's just fun). We self-medicate with booze or gaming or binge watching *The Bounty Hunter*. That's why resilient leaders must practice happiness.

Practice it? Yes, practice. Happiness is an emotion and, like all emotions, it ebbs and flows. The feeling of happiness is fleeting so we need to practice it continually to have more moments of peace and calm. As Don Draper from the hit TV show, *Madmen*, said, "What is happiness except the moment before you need more happiness?" The more moments you have, the more you are building up your resiliency to be able to better handle life when the crap sandwich shows up on your plate.

In her book, *The How of Happiness*, Dr. Sonja Lyubormirsky researched the conditions for which people were happy. She found that nearly 50% of our overall happiness in life is genetically preconditioned. In that, we get it from our parents. (If you're not that happy, blame your folks.) Only 10% of our overall happiness is due to our circumstances and thus the other 40% comes from things we can do to make ourselves either more or less happy.

Think about that for a minute. Only 10% of my happiness is due to the crap that is hurled at me. I have a choice on getting past the crap and being happier. I can't blame Mom and Dad, or my job, or my boss, or my spouse, or the weather, or my losing sports team. If I have a shitty disposition, it's under my control.

So why is all this crap making me so unhappy? It could be I'm not practicing happiness effectively; it could be I'm filling the hole with more crap.

When I was facing crap and not practicing happiness (and the other steps of this book), one of my go-to crap hole fillers was work. I've worked all my life. I got my first paper route in the fourth grade and haven't stopped working since. After my first divorce from my ex-wife, we didn't have any children yet, nothing else to fill my time, and work became a source of comfort for me. I wrapped myself up in my job and work worked for filling the hole. But that isn't always the case. Sometimes work becomes the wrong band aid to help the chafing.

Before and after September 11th, 2001 were trying times for me. As I shared before, I was in a big job with big responsibilities. Instead of trying to fill the hole that the crap had created with the right things, I filled it with more work which created more crap. My ex and I had re-married several years prior and now had four kids. Things were not so great at home because I was never there. And, even when I was there, I still wasn't there. My wife was mad at me for never being around. My kids were mad at me for never being around. I was mad at me, but my default coping mechanism was work.

What are your go-to band aids that help you fill the hole caused by crap? After a recent workshop on this topic, one woman shared with me that her go-to was binge shopping. Another man at a different program shared with me that his go-to was drinking. Please note that I love a good vodka tonic (heavy on the vodka and light on the tonic) but if it's your band aid, it's only going to make things worse.

For the woman with binge shopping, she ended up with buyer's remorse and more crap from her husband for her spending habits. For the man, drinking gave him an evening of respite from the rigors of the day only to find out he had made a complete ass of himself while doing it. The point is that we all have band aids. Don't reach for the wrong ones, choose to do something different.

> **CRAPTASTIC FACT**
>
> THE MORE ADEPT YOU BECOME AT A SKILL, THE LESS WORK YOUR BRAIN HAS TO DO. OVER TIME, A SKILL BECOMES AUTOMATIC AND YOU DON'T NEED TO THINK ABOUT WHAT YOU'RE DOING. THIS IS BECAUSE YOUR BRAIN IS ACTUALLY STRENGTHENING ITSELF OVER TIME AS YOU LEARN THAT SKILL.

I am not a proponent of the concept of work/life balance. Balancing would infer that I'm giving equal time to all the things in my life. What I am a proponent of is practice.

One practice that helps me get past the crap is to take care of myself first. Now, I am not one of those people to stand on a soapbox and preach on the resiliency benefits of a good diet, sleep, and exercise. These are all things that I work on constantly. Having grown up a fat kid, I can tell you that I love food and have a love/hate relationship with exercise. I go through spurts on all of them. Actually, it's my daughter, Abby, that told me that I'd never have to go on a diet ever if I just knew about one word…moderation. I don't know anything about moderation. When I'm on a diet, I'm on. When I'm in an exercise routine, I'm obsessive. When I'm not, it's donuts and Netflix! YEAH!

Taking care of myself first can entail the right sleep, exercise and eating habits. But, mostly, it's thinking of my needs in addition to the others around me. Do you take care of your own needs? Or are you too busy tending to everyone else?

I love the way my daughter, Victoria, looks at life. I'd like to think she takes after me in her views, but some are completely hers. She has a bunch of little phrases she uses for advice to her three siblings. One of which, "You gotta do you, boo," was given to her younger sister when Abby was facing a conundrum of what to do when facing two options.

YOU GOTTA DO YOU, BOO! Hell yes, we all gotta do us because no one else is going to.

How many times have you put everyone and everything else ahead of what you really need? That usually just causes more stress for you in the long run. Doing me first is a firm practice that helps me handle the rigors of any day. Whether it's getting enough sleep or saying no to a request, I have to take care of this boo first.

When I was filling the hole with more work, what I should have been doing is practicing being where I was, fully. I interviewed a top basketball performance coach for my podcast (www.leadershiphappyhour.com) and what he shared is that, no matter where he is, his mind is where his feet are. Had I actually been present and in the moment when not at work, I wouldn't have been borrowing from Peter to pay Paul and pissing Peter (my wife) off. I would have been being mindful and paying attention to Peter when Peter was present. Paul's turn will come. Mindfulness is a practice and an incredibly helpful band aid we all can use to help the chafing.

Nick Mostca, founder of Personalized Mindfulness, states that mindfulness is the process of entering into the present moment and choosing a skillful response to what we experience. We have to recognize that we are not our stress or the problems we face. Mindfulness is like entering into the eye of a storm where you have a better perspective on all the stress swirling around you.

Be mindful of where you are, who are with, and what is going on around you. It's an ongoing practice and you will see the rewards.

We humans also need other humans. Looking back on why work worked for me after my first divorce, it was partly that work helped take my mind off how my relationship had ended but more so, it helped me be social. Since I had no children then and no family around, the people at work became my family. Resilient leaders don't isolate themselves. They practice being social. Yes, practice.

A new study found that belonging to a social group helps to alleviate depression. And, it appears the closer the tie to the group, the better the results. Psychologists Dr. Alexander Haslam and Dr. Tegan Cruwys and their colleagues at the University of Queensland conducted two studies of patients diagnosed with depression or anxiety.

The patients either joined a community group with activities such as sewing, yoga, sports, or art, or partook in group therapy at a psychiatric hospital. In both cases, when responding to survey questions, patients who did not identify strongly with the social group they were in had about a 50 percent likelihood of continued depression a month later. But of those who developed a stronger connection to the group and who came to see its members as "us" rather than "them," less than a third still met the criteria for clinical depression. Many patients said the group made them feel supported because everyone was "in it together."

> ACCORDING TO *PSYCHOLOGY TODAY*, EVERY THOUGHT RELEASES BRAIN CHEMICALS. "THINKING POSITIVE, HAPPY, HOPEFUL, OPTIMISTIC, JOYFUL THOUGHTS DECREASES CORTISOL AND PRODUCES SEROTONIN, WHICH CREATES A SENSE OF WELL—BEING. THIS HELPS YOUR BRAIN FUNCTION AT PEAK CAPACITY."

We, as humans, need interaction. Make the choice to seek out something social to do with a group you identify with. When you spend time with others, you want it to be enjoyable and feel a connection. When I do this, I kill two birds with one stone. I get social and I do so with a group that pays it forward. Giving back (or serving something larger than yourself) is a practice that takes your mind off you and your woes.

After my second divorce (I married and divorced the same woman twice), I was in a funk. My finances were jacked, I missed my kids, and I couldn't seem to see the light at the end of the tunnel. With now being self-employed and not having a social outlet at work, I isolated myself and made myself more miserable.

That was until I got a call from the Pastor at a church I frequented. They needed someone to head up the community meal that the church supported, and she asked if I would be willing to take that on. My first response in my head was to say no. I wasn't in any mood to be around other people. I was too busy feeling sorry for myself. But, instead, I said yes (going back to being pliable and trying something new). The result was not only therapeutic in fulfilling my social needs, the act of giving back filled the hole I had with happiness.

Research has shown that giving makes us much happier than receiving. Studies have shown that giving money to others or to charity will put a much bigger smile on your face than spending on yourself. Michael Norton, a professor at Harvard Business School, conducted one such study.

With his colleagues, Norton questioned 632 Americans about their level of income and what they spent their money on. They were also asked to rate their own happiness. North found that, regardless of income, those who spent money on others were decidedly happier than those who spent more on themselves. Have no extra money? Give your time.

> **CRAPTASTIC FACT**
>
> GIVING BACK HAS AN EFFECT ON YOUR BODY. STUDIES SHOW THAT WHEN PEOPLE DONATED TO CHARITY, THE MESOLIMBIC SYSTEM, THE PORTION OF THE BRAIN RESPONSIBLE FOR FEELINGS OF REWARD, WAS TRIGGERED. THE BRAIN ALSO RELEASES FEEL-GOOD CHEMICALS AND SPURS YOU TO PERFORM MORE KIND ACTS — SOMETHING PSYCHOLOGISTS CALL "HELPER'S HIGH."

As a side note, running the community meal also gave me some perspective. No matter what kind of crap was going on in my life, there are others that have it worse. It's all relative. Want some perspective and you don't have time to volunteer? Watch the Jerry Springer show. That will give you some perspective and make you VERY grateful for your own life.

Gratitude? Yes, another practice that promotes happiness. Science has shown that finding one thing to be thankful for from your previous day and remembering it in your current day can do wonders in elevating your overall mood.

But let's face it, when the crap is heavy, gratitude is a band aid that can be elusive. What do you do on those days? Focus in on the little things.

We all have something to be thankful for, regardless of our circumstances. Maybe it's the fact that the sun is shining. Perhaps it's that your spouse is making your favorite meal. Or, it could even be as simple as getting a good cup of coffee.

A few years ago, I was on my way to Oklahoma City to speak for a convention and my flight got interrupted by a storm. The connection I had through Dallas got diverted to Austin and we sat on the runway for four hours waiting to take off. When I finally got to Dallas, it was a madhouse. Everyone was hustling around, trying to get a flight, and angry because they weren't going anywhere. I wasn't any different. I was the kickoff speaker the next day and I needed to get there by noon in order to fulfill my obligation.

After standing in line (for what seemed like) two hours, I finally got to the agent who informed me that they didn't know if they'd get me out of there for two days. WHAT!? I was furious. While lying in my hotel room (yes, I was lucky enough to have that and should have been grateful), all I could do was ruminate about the predicament I was in. Then I made a choice. I couldn't control anything that was going on here and I was making myself crazy. I decided to just focus on getting a good cup of coffee in the AM. After that, what happens, happens.

The next morning had me up early to get the airport. When I walked in, it looked like a homeless shelter. People were sleeping everywhere. On chairs, on the floor, and on top of each other. And, in the distance, I saw the subtle green glow of a Starbucks. YES! The cup of coffee I wanted. I got it and as I sipped it, I let the gratitude of that moment cover me like a warm blanket on a cold winter day. I then sauntered over to the ticket counter and met the agent as he was coming on duty. "So, what do you think? Can I get out of here and get to OKC today?" I asked.

"Let me check, Mr. Lutz."

I sipped and smiled.

"Well, actually," he looked up at me, "we have a flight boarding right now. Would you like to get that one?"

HELL YES! I thought (and may have actually said).

The rest of the day went like clockwork. I got the flight, had a shuttle waiting as soon as I landed and got to my speaking engagement with 30 minutes to spare. Why? I believe it's because I made a choice to grab the right band aid. I went for gratitude instead of despair and anger. It calmed me, got me past the crap I couldn't control, and bounced me back into action.

> **CRAPTASTIC FACT**
>
> GRATEFUL PEOPLE EXPERIENCE FEWER ACHES AND PAINS AND THEY REPORT FEELING HEALTHIER THAN OTHER PEOPLE, ACCORDING TO A 2012 STUDY PUBLISHED IN *PERSONALITY AND INDIVIDUAL DIFFERENCES*. NOT SURPRISINGLY, GRATEFUL PEOPLE ARE ALSO MORE LIKELY TO TAKE CARE OF THEIR HEALTH, WHICH IS LIKELY TO CONTRIBUTE TO FURTHER LONGEVITY.

Focus on what you can control, or what you can't control will control you. It's always your choice and gratitude is always under your control. It's the little things we can be grateful for that can give us the moment of happiness we need. One moment can shift perspective and get us past the crap.

The last practice that helps me, more than anything, is to try to find the meaning behind whatever crap I'm going through. If I can find the meaning, I can learn and grow.

In 1942, prominent Jewish psychiatrist, Victor Frankl, was arrested and taken to a Nazi concentration camp. After his three-year ordeal there was over and he was liberated, he found that most of his family (including his pregnant wife) were gone. In his internationally acclaimed book, *Man's Search for Meaning,* he wrote about his experiences in the camps and concluded that the difference between those who lived and those who died in the camps came down to one thing: meaning.

Current research has shown that finding the meaning in life and giving back improves our overall mental health, builds esteem, and enhances resiliency.

I left this practice for last in this chapter because I think the other practices help me put my mind in a place that is more apt to find meaning. I think the opposite is also true. When I'm looking for meaning, I am more apt to be mindful of what is going on, find the thing to be thankful for, and not fill the hole with crap. Meaning leads to hope and hope is the springboard for getting over all the crap.

BEING A RESILIENT LEADER IS A PRACTICE. ARE YOU WILLING?

GET PAST THE CRAP!

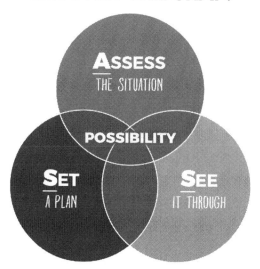

ASSESS YOUR CURRENT SITUATION

Where are you on the Craptometer scale?

LEVEL 1	LEVEL 2	LEVEL 3	LEVEL 4
Everything is **CRAPTASTIC!**	Same Old **CRAP**	**CRAP** is getting **HEAVY**	My Life is **CRAP**

ARE YOU WILLING TO IMPLEMENT THE PRACTICES NECESSARY TO GET PAST YOUR CRAP?

- What are filling your hole with?
- What band aids do you reach for?

SET A PLAN

1. How are you taking care of yourself first?
2. What are 3 things you are currently grateful for?
3. What social activities can you participate in that also give back?
4. What is some crap you've gone through in the past that has, in the end, made you a better person (meaning)?

SEE IT THROUGH

Write down specific concrete actions:

Today, I will _____
_____.

This week, I will _____
_____.

This month, I will _____
_____.

WRITE DOWN YOUR POSSIBILITY:

_____
_____
_____
_____
_____
_____
_____
_____
_____
_____
_____
_____
_____
_____
_____
_____
_____
_____
_____
_____

CHAPTER 7

GET PAST THE CRAP WITH
PLAY

"When you're in jail, a good friend will be trying to bail you out. A best friend will be in the cell next to you saying, 'Damn, that was fun'."

–Malcolm Gladwell

Remember back when you sat in school, studying or doing vocabulary, and you couldn't wait for that time of day when you got a respite from the churnings and burnings of the classroom and got to go out for recess? YES, RECESS! A time for fun. A time for laughing. A time for play. There wasn't any stress with recess (unless the bully you made fun of earlier that day threatened to beat you up at recess (true story)). Remember what it was like to cut loose and just decompress? You still need to do that. Resilient leaders get past their crap with play!

George Bernard Shaw said, "We don't stop playing because we get old, we get old because we stop playing." Research has shown that playful adults have the ability to transform everyday situations, even stressful ones, into something entertaining.

Further, play serves as the catalyst for everything else we've talked about in this book.

Play is finding the humor in a humorless situation. Sharing a joke with a friend. Laughing so hard milk squirts out your nose. It's more than just playing a game; play is the freedom to express yourself and relieve yourself of the crap that happens every day.

We all know that shit happens, and I'm here to remind you that play needs to as well. As a leader, a little play can reap some hefty returns if used strategically.

Play makes you likeable. Let's face it; there are a lot of things that leaders have to do that put us in the not-liked-so-much arena. That doesn't mean that you personally aren't liked. There's a big difference between you being likeable and some of your responsibilities not being adored by your team. The strategic use of humor makes you more likeable and gives you the referent power base you need (that's where people want to do things because of your sheer awesome magnitude rather than you telling them they have to).

Play reduces team stress. In the Navy, they say that the Captain is the ship. This has a lot of different connotations, but I see it to mean that the people in the department take on the personality of the person in charge. They also adapt to the Captain's emotional state. If you're stressed out, you can bet that your team will be stressed out. Laughing at issues changes the emotional state and makes things less stressful. About ONE

MILLION workers EACH DAY take time off due to stress related complaints. Don't you think a little play can have some impact?

Play encourages innovation. Humor is freedom. Leaders that can laugh at their own mistakes in essence give permission to their people to do the same. The team will no longer be encumbered with worrying of making a misstep. They know that if their leader can laugh and be humble, so can they, and then find the learning. Today's competitive world needs people that aren't afraid to make a mistake. They'll take your lead.

Play enhances engagement. What enthralls you more: working in a sterile environment, or one where people enjoy what they're doing and who they're with? I think the latter (unless you're an undertaker). According to the Harvard Business Review, "Laughter relieves stress and boredom, boosts engagement and well-being, and spurs not only creativity and collaboration but also analytic precision and productivity." That is what leaders and teams all want.

Play reduces turnover. Teams that play together, stay together. Why would you want to leave your friends and workplace that is fun? Glassdoor, a job and recruiting website that holds a large database of more than 8 million company reviews, has found that the top companies create a fun, collaborative work environment that place a strong emphasis on employee empowerment and enjoyment. Employee retention is good for moral and the bottom line.

PLAY BUILDS COHESIVE TEAMS.

The best teams I have been on were where we worked hard and we played hard. No one complained when we did both at the same time, either. Most teams develop a sense of humor of their own that outside teams don't understand. That's because they've been in the trenches together, and have shared experiences. Those bonds are hard to break. Further, fun-natured competition inspires more innovation and begets more bonding too.

Play can curb bad behavior and enforce norms. A little gentle ribbing about something that is out of the norm has a greater impact on curbing deviant behavior than a reprimand. A team member may take the lead in pointing out misbehavior and save the leader the stress of the situation. Play encourages trust.

Play is fun. Fun is its own reward. As humans, we're built to play. It's a part of our DNA. As we grow up we look at play as the opposite of work and that's poppycock. Even if the task itself is not that great, if the environment is fun, I'm in (aren't you?).

> **CRAPTASTIC FACT**
>
> JUST 10 TO 15 MINUTES OF LAUGHING A DAY CAN BURN UP TO 40 CALORIES, ACCORDING TO A VANDERBILT UNIVERSITY STUDY. RESEARCHERS DETERMINED THAT THE INCREASE IN HEART RATE AND OXYGEN CONSUMPTION DURING THESE FUNNY MOMENTS BOOSTED THE BURN.

Play can also help you with maintaining your purpose. My dad worked in a steel mill and hated every day of it. His sense of family and responsibility was his purpose. At times, he worked three jobs to make ends meet. Never complaining, he raised us all with a strong work ethic, sense of family and most importantly a sense of humor. If it hadn't been for his sense of humor, I believe that the stresses of the jobs and all of us kids would've killed him. The legacy he provided of seeing the humorous side of things has helped me throughout my entire life, and has truly been the recipe for success in my professional life. For twenty-two years in the Navy and since retiring from that great organization, I've built on that foundation and learned that if you want to stay, you've got to play.

A little play can help you with pliability. Let's face it; we live in a world of change. What stresses us out is the loss of control and that we can't predict what's going to happen. Play and humor makes the scary less scary. Some issues we face seem larger than ourselves or what we can deal with. When we can laugh at the issue, it decreases in psychological size. It becomes smaller. It no longer controls us, we control it. Dr. John Morreall, a professor of Philosophy at the college of William and Mary, wrote that "humor is freedom…and incompatible with fear."

When facing a tough situation, I'll play the *What If?* game. What if my boss wasn't an ass and wore a tutu to work? What if I wasn't broke and money did grow on trees? What if the constitution was changed and Schwarzenegger could be President? The "what if?" makes me laugh and puts me in the driver's seat.

Asking, "What if?" allows me to play with the situation, find the humor and humor gives control.

Play can shift our perspective and can make change seem less risky. Have you ever been so close to a problem that you can't see it from any other view? Playing with the situation and looking at the circumstances humorously turns everything on its side and opens up a whole new world of possibilities. Allen Klein, in his classic book *The Healing Power of Humor* wrote that "Humor lends a fresh eye…when we can find some humor in our upsets, they no longer seem as large or as important as they once did."

Parallel to my *What If?* exercise for gaining perspective, I use the *What's the Worst that Can Happen?* game in order to get a new view (using play and humor) in confronting an issue. It's either going work out like I want, or it's not. If not, what's the funny "worse that can happen?" For instance, I speak to large groups of people for a living. If it goes great, they cheer my name and throw roses at me. If not, what's the worst that could happen? They rant my name and throw flaming bags of poo at me (which by the way, has never happened). Finding a humorous "what's the worst" scenario makes me laugh and laughing puts it ALL in perspective. And yes, you should book me to speak at your next function (shameless plug.)

Humor and play allows us to cope. A good friend of mine served in Iraq during the height of the war surge. Part of his duties were to coordinate with the morgue in getting fallen soldiers back home to the US. In his first dealings with the junior soldiers that were working there, he was appalled that they would joke around while working. Later, after reflecting on it, he realized humor was the only way they could deal with the horrific job they had. Many of the bodies they prepped were people that they knew, their friends. Humor gave them the emotional distance they needed to do that job. It wasn't out of disrespect; it was the necessary means to an end. Humor can be dark but it is in the darkness that humor brings us into the light.

> **CRAPTASTIC FACT:** RESEARCH SHOWS THAT COUPLES WHO USE LAUGHTER AND SMILE WHEN DISCUSSING A TOUCHY SUBJECT FEEL BETTER IN THE IMMEDIACY AND REPORT HIGHER LEVELS OF SATISFACTION IN THEIR RELATIONSHIP. THEY ALSO TEND TO STAY TOGETHER LONGER.

Every young recruit is shipped off to boot camp to become formally "indoctrinated" into the organization. To get a clear picture of what the first week is like, imagine yourself spending every waking hour and sleeping hour with 80 sweaty, young, stinky, and homesick men. This is while two "seasoned sailors" called Company Commanders, your "acclimators," spend their time finding new ways to torture you (okay, it's not really torture in the Geneva Convention sense of it). To complete the picture, add a dash of learning your left from your right, a sprinkle of (what was fondly termed) the recruit crud (a nasty cold), and a dollop of speaking in acronyms, and you have a great recipe for stress. Some young soldiers crack and go home; some get serious; and some, like me, cope with humor.

One example happened during "mail call." I had just received a letter from my mother. Among her other updates was a mention that a classmate from high school had been crowned Miss Illinois and that, if I had a chance, I should watch her compete in the Miss America pageant. That, in and of itself, was funny. Regardless, I decided to ask the question. I went to my Company Commander and said "Sir, my mom said that, if I got the chance, I should watch the Miss America pageant on TV. You see, a classmate of mine…" and that's where he stopped me.

"Lutz," he said, "I can't believe you!"

"Well," I replied, "it says in the Bible to 'ask and ye shall receive… I was just being holy."

"It didn't say what you would receive! Give me 50 pushups!" he bellowed and then started laughing.

We all started laughing. In the end, it was this, among other incongruous statements I would make, that I am sure caused him to remember me and recommend me for meritorious promotion to the next grade when I left.

Finding the humor in the darkness isn't always easy but it can work. After my divorce, I put my ex-wife's picture on a dart board and charged my co-workers a dollar a dart to help me pay for my divorce. Was that dark humor? You bet, but it helped me cope. Humor made the crappy, less crappy. It'll help you too.

> **CRAPTASTIC FACT**
>
> PEOPLE THAT APPRECIATE DARK HUMOR ARE SHARPER THAN AVERAGE. STUDIES HAVE FOUND THESE INDIVIDUALS MORE EMOTIONALLY STABLE, HAPPIER, AND BETTER ADJUSTED. THEY ARE ABLE TO DISTANCE THEMSELVES FROM TOPICS THAT OTHERS MIGHT FIND TABOO.

Play and a little humor can make tough conversations more fluid and facilitate better communication. Life is full of tough conversations, especially as a leader.

One of my first supervisors in the Navy was great at injecting humor. Regardless of what fire was being extinguished (usually due to a mistake I made), he'd find the humor in it and share. It put both of us at ease and then we could find the learning from the situation. He could've yelled and had an angry outburst (it was certainly warranted) but he chose a different route where I'd be more receptive. When people are angry, their ears are off. It was Herbert Gardner that said, "When people are laughing, they're listening."

When I joined the senior Petty Officer ranks in the Navy, I was selected for a job as an inspector and I was very excited about the opportunity. Thanks to a positive attitude and not taking myself too seriously, I had always done well, but this position was a little different. I decided that I was going to hit this job with all I had and really make a difference. I was going to buckle down and get serious because many would be counting on me for accurate information and they didn't want it from a jokester. They wanted it from one of those serious guys with the glasses who knew everything. Yes, a load of crap I heaped on myself.

When I reported aboard, I found it was a serious command. The Commodore was a very quiet man who would, when spoken to, sit and reflect on your statements before commenting. He took in everything said to him and always responded very literally. I found that, even though I tried hard, I couldn't be that serious guy with the glasses who knew everything. I studied and knew a lot, but I had to be me. Me...with everyone but the Commodore.

The Commodore frightened me in a way. My off-the-cuff remarks would sometimes be taken at face value--which was neither funny nor was it understood. I found myself feeling very uncomfortable and trying to be something that I wasn't when the Commodore was around. In short, I was miserable. I was at a loss as to how to handle the situation, or myself, so I called my previous boss and asked for his advice. His advice was simple. He said, "Just be yourself. You are your best asset....hell, I didn't like you at first until I got to know you." I sat and thought about it. He was right.

I decided to change it right then. Luckily, that afternoon, the opportunity arose and I went for it. I was standing in the office eating a bag of "Utz" brand potato chips. The Commodore walked through and I acknowledged him, and then pointed at the bag and then me and said "Utz....Lutz".

I said, "Sir, did you know that my great grandmother started the Utz potato chip line in her basement at the turn of the century?"

This caught his attention; he stopped and said, "No," and waited for me to finish. I continued, "Yes, she started it and they were a huge success. Something about the oil she used. Anyway, as time moved on she became concerned about how this new wealth would affect the family. Great-Grandma Lutz was, after all, starting to amass a small fortune and it was right around the time of the Lindbergh kidnappings. So, she decided to change the name to protect the family, you know, ... ' Get the "L" out of there.'"

He stood there for a minute (reflecting as usual), looked at me, shook his head and chuckled and then went to his office. It was the only time I ever saw him laugh--even a little bit! That was the turning point in our work relationship. More importantly, it taught me that there's a lot of crap we make for ourselves and if you want to be successful, you gotta break it down with a laugh.

I always have a joke on the ready. If jokes aren't your thing, try the "you don't see (or hear or witness) that every day" phrase when something is amiss and tension needs to be averted. Just don't do it with your wife's cooking. It does, however, work with ugly babies. "You don't see a baby like that every day!"

A little humor won't give you 100% stress-free communication, but it will certainly help grease the skids for something worthwhile. Playful curiosity can help you with pliability as well. It's like turning the crank on the jack-in-the-box and waiting for it to pop out. You know it's going to, but you don't know when and, when it does, it usually results in laughing.

> AN INDUSTRY—WIDE STUDY OF OVER 2,500 PEOPLE FOUND THAT 55% OF WORKERS WOULD TAKE LESS PAY TO HAVE MORE FUN AT WORK. THIS MEANS A MAJORITY OF PEOPLE WOULD LITERALLY TAKE A PAY CUT FOR A MORE LIGHT—HEARTED WORK ENVIRONMENT.

If you look at Einstein or Mozart, or other creative geniuses, their life was made up of imaginative manipulation of narratives, mathematical symbols, sounds and notes, colors or forms. They found true joy in their being using imaginative capacities by playing with the objects they loved. Einstein said that, "Imagination is more important than knowledge."

Be proactive in being playful and finding the humor in all that you do. Play and humor can help you practice keeping your mind on the things that are truly important. At one point in my career, my workforce was short, funding was shorter, and tasks were numerous. I left my house at 3:30am and didn't get home until late. Even then, I was still consumed by what I had to get done and what wasn't getting done. I lost my fun factor; I had a job to do, people to lead and had become that guy--the one who is really serious and works all the time.

This lasted for nearly a year until one day, my then-wife called me and said, "I overheard the kids upstairs planning a mutiny. They said that they are tired of you being gone and working all the time. They're going to give you one more week to get it together or they're leaving."

I stopped, thought a moment, and then started laughing. The thought of those little boogers planning a mutiny (in my head they were wearing little pirate hats and carrying wooden swords (one had a peg leg)) is what brought me back from the depths of seriousness to who I really am. I had plunged deep but all it took was a really good laugh to get me back to me. Granted, it took a lot to get back into their good graces (not really, children are pretty forgiving) but we got back on track. It just took a look at things through their eyes so I could see the funny.

I'm at a point in my life now that if something's not fun I don't want to do it. And, if I do have to do it, I'm going to work to make it as enjoyable as possible. But I had a time when I say that humor literally saved my life.

Long story short, my wife had affairs which caused our divorce. We married again and had four amazing kids and I thought all that crap was behind us. Our children were all ages ten and younger when my wife was shipped out of town (she was a Navy Reservist).

Two weeks into her absence, I could feel that something was different in our relationship. The calls were less frequent, there was an apathy in her voice, and certain things she told me didn't really make sense (on being one place and then telling me something different later…stuff like that). It all seemed so familiar. These were the exact feelings I had when she had her previous affairs. Her behavior felt the same and I started the internal dialogue the spurred me into a stress spiral. I drove myself nuts. I couldn't control what was going on there so I took it out on myself. I couldn't eat (in 45 days I lost 30 pounds). I was morose and moped around. I finally decided that I needed to go see for myself what was going on.

When I landed at the airport, there she was to greet me, nervous and a bit jittery. We cautiously embraced and she took me back to where she was staying. She was the same person, but something seemed different. Was it the fact she was missing the kids and put on a brave face? Was it something else?

That whole week was a barrage of arguments. Finally, it all came to a head. She had, in fact, cheated again. Having my suspicions confirmed certainly didn't make me feel any better. I was a wreck. I felt like a stranger to my wife, and to myself. I was in a strange country, in a strange hotel and was spiraling out of control. I was at the lowest I had ever been in my life.

I decided to go for a walk and wandered aimlessly forever and ended up at a train station. Standing on the edge, being on edge, I had that moment that no one ever thinks will happen to them, but as I have since found out, happens to many of us. As the train turned the corner and came my way, I thought, "All I have to do is just step. Just step in front and all of this pain is gone. I won't have to deal with anything anymore. I won't have to feel anything anymore. All I have to do is step."

Of course, I didn't step. I thought of my kids and instead of stepping in front of the train, I decided to step onto the train. I didn't know where it was going but anyplace was better than where I was.

The train, two stops down, brought me to a shopping center that had a movie theater. Yes, something to take my mind off what was going on. The movie I got to see was Old School, with Will Ferrell. If you've seen the movie, then you probably know that it is one of the dumbest movies ever made. But, it made me laugh. It made me smile. The idiotic antics on the movie were like a helicopter that lifted me up over the issues I was currently facing and helped me realize that I could get through this, I would get through this. And I did.

When I got back to the hotel, it was the same crap sandwich but my perspective was different. I changed my ticket and left the next day. I don't tell you all this to bash my ex-wife. I share it to show the power of humor and how it, literally, saved my life. In that moment, I made a choice to do something different. I chose to put a little play into play. In every single moment, even when it may not seem like it, we always have a choice. That is my point in this book and in getting so personal here. We have a choice, and we always do better when we face our crap head on. Option 3, remember?

When working on my Master's Thesis, I interviewed Father John Naus, a priest who taught a class on humor at Marquette University in Milwaukee. The words he shared have stayed with me: "Humor renders people benevolent."

Humor rendered me benevolent to myself. It pulled me from the depths and helped me push past the crap and go on to create an amazing life. As you can see, humor and play aren't just for children. You need it too. The power is in your hands, no matter what crap is on your plate, take a deep breath and a big bite, and go out and play.

GET PAST THE CRAP!

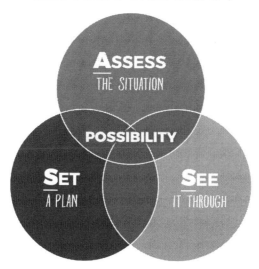

ASSESS YOUR CURRENT SITUATION

Where are you on the Craptometer scale?

LEVEL 1	LEVEL 2	LEVEL 3	LEVEL 4
Everything is **CRAPTASTIC!**	Same Old **CRAP**	**CRAP** is getting **HEAVY**	My Life is **CRAP**

ARE YOU WILLING TO PLAY?

- Are you laughing enough?
- Is there joy in your day to day activities? Why or why not?

SET A PLAN

1. What do you do to decompress?
2. How do you incorporate play with your team?
3. Do you make a point to laugh every day—at work and at home?
4. How can you be more benevolent to yourself and play more?

SEE IT THROUGH

Write down specific concrete actions:

Today, I will _____
_____.

This week, I will _____
_____.

This month, I will _____
_____.

WRITE DOWN YOUR POSSIBILITY:

CHAPTER 8

GET PAST THE BY
TAKING THE PLEDGE

"Fear is the loneliest feeling. You can be in a throng of people, but if you're afraid, you're on your own."
–Michelle Paver

"When you raise your right hand and give your oath, you're just not enlisting yourself, you're enlisting your entire family and also your support community." Those were the words I said to the group of enlistees when I gave my daughter, Victoria, her oath of enlistment into the Army a few years ago. The same rings true when you choose Option 3 and decide to take that crap sandwich head-on. You're not just making a choice for you; you are causing a ripple effect that will impact your family, your team, and your community. That's why resilient leaders make a pledge to not get in their own way.

Pledging to get out of your own way is a pledge to subscribe to a way of life. Habits aren't that hard to form; what it takes is consistency and commitment. According to the website, Lifehack, three to four weeks is all the time you need to make a habit automatic. If you can make it through the initial conditioning phase, a new habit becomes much easier to sustain. A month is a good block of time to commit to a change since it easily fits in your calendar. Here, they were talking about physical conditioning, but (with the strategies/steps in this book) you're conditioning your mind and the same is true.

Ever started the new year with resolutions? According to *Psychology Today,* nearly 50% of the population does. But, even so, 80% of them fail within the first two weeks. It's not because of laziness, it's because they aren't thinking strategically and acting tactically (go back to the chapter on purpose).

You know where you want to be, but your daily habits have to be in alignment with being crap-free. Put the daily action steps in place to be positive. That's why at the end of each chapter, there's a "See it through…today, I will" section. Even if the steps are small, you'll still get there if you're committed to getting past the crap.

The reason we pledge to get out of our own way is that often we can be the biggest barrier to our own success in getting something done. When there is something I know I need to do, I can come up with every excuse in the book to keep from doing it.

Two months into my first Command tour, the call came in. The call I never wanted to receive. I had to make a Next of Kin notification to a mother to let her know that her son (who was serving in the Navy) was dead. I knew that was a part of my job. Being the only Navy base in Kansas, it was a duty that they had covered in Commanding Officer school, but one that I had hoped would never come.

I don't like giving bad news. As a leader, it's a part of my job but not something I enjoy. This was a different kind of bad news. This wasn't telling someone they weren't getting promoted, or giving an adverse performance appraisal. This was very personal for me. As a father of four, I couldn't ever imagine receiving that kind of news and it definitely wasn't something I wanted to give.

The first order of business was to find someone to go with you. Part of the protocol is to make the notification as quickly as possible and to never go alone. I called over to the Chaplain's office at McConnell Air Force Base and, luckily, found a Chaplain that was available to go with me that morning.

When I picked him up, he could tell the distress I was feeling and filled the deafening silence with chit chat about me and where I was from. We drove to the mother's house and no one was home. A quick wave of relief came over me but, even so, it was momentary. I knew that the mission was still ahead of me. We drove to her place of work, a local middle school, only to find that we had just missed her. Her co-workers were curious as to why we were there and I knew that we needed to act quickly in order to get this done properly. Within the Navy, we pride ourselves on taking care of our own. Next of Kin notifications are always done within 24 hours and always by us. We never want a loved one to find out from the grapevine or on the phone from someone outside of the Navy. We do it and work to be there for the family throughout the process to help with their transition.

We quickly went back to the mother's house. I saw a car in the driveway and knew she was home. My mouth was dry, my heart was racing, and I had white knuckles on the steering wheel from grabbing it so tightly in tension. I parked, slowly got out of the car and the Chaplain and I walked slowly up to the house. At the edge of the sidewalk leading up to the front door, I stopped. My internal dialogue was telling me I couldn't do this. I wasn't this guy. I didn't give this kind of news. I felt immobilized with the stress of the moment.

That's when the Chaplain said, "Lieutenant Lutz, you need to step out of your own way on this. This isn't about you and you not wanting to do this; it's about taking care of our own and being there for that mother. Now step out of your own way."

His words put my feet back into motion and we made it to the front door. I will spare you the intimate details but, in the end, the job was done and, after the shock and despair subsided, the mother and I became friends as I helped her get through one her life's most trying times.

> **CRAPTASTIC FACT**
>
> KINDNESS IS CONTAGIOUS, ACCORDING TO A STUDY BY RESEARCHERS AT UNIVERSITY OF CALIFORNIA—LOS ANGELES, AND BY THE UNIVERSITY OF CAMBRIDGE AND UNIVERSITY OF PLYMOUTH IN THE UNITED KINGDOM. "WHEN WE SEE SOMEONE ELSE HELP ANOTHER PERSON IT GIVES US A GOOD FEELING," THE STUDY STATES, "WHICH IN TURN CAUSES US TO GO OUT AND DO SOMETHING ALTRUISTIC OURSELVES."

Crap can immobilize us to the point where we can't take a step and we are standing in our own way in moving forward. What is the crap that gets keeps us stuck in our own path? Fear, holding on to the past, resentment and myriad other self-defeating shit storms.

Fear can also keep us from stepping out and taking the risk that we know we should take. Getting past the crap involves taking a risk, trying something different.

I have as many fear issues as anyone. Having grown up a plump Lutz, most of my fears stem from the insecurities I learned in the classroom. Those of looking stupid, sounding dumb or not being "good enough." As a leader, those issues still rear their ugly head when I need to do something that is scary and could (if left unattended) stagnate me (and my team) in a pool of "could have been."

If I'm looking to step out of my own way, the first thing I need to do is to quit worrying. Worry about the "what ifs" is a huge fear for most. "What if this? What if that?" are common objections to taking action. I always think of the line from *Wayne's World*: "What if monkeys fly out of my butt?" Worry solves nothing, action does. 95% of what we worry about never happens and the other 5% doesn't matter. And, if you're worried about the accuracy of my statistic, don't be. I made it up…but find it to be true. Worry is crap.

> "BY SITTING AND MINDFULLY BREATHING FOR 10 MINUTES A DAY, IN AS LITTLE AS EIGHT WEEKS YOU STRENGTHEN THE PART OF THE PRE-FRONTAL CORTEX INVOLVED IN GENERATING POSITIVE FEELINGS AND DIMINISH THE PART THAT GENERATES NEGATIVE ONES."
> RICHARD DAVIDSON, PHD.)

I have a coaching client, Ron, who is a chronic worrier. I get that. I am too. My mom says it's genetic and that I get it from my father. Ron's worries usually centered around what his boss thought about him, what his team thought about him, if he was doing the right thing, etc. Not only did it strip the joy out his daily life, his constant fretting also kept Ron from making decisions. This nagging worry caused Ron to keep from living and enjoying what was going on around him. He had to take the pledge to step out of his own way. Ron was keeping himself from getting past the crap.

Apply the same advice I give myself when I'm immobilized by worry and fear: take a deep breath and acknowledge the crap but don't let it own you. Invoke Option 3 and take a big bite. Dr. Chad Lejeune in his book, *The Worry Trap,* says that one great step to overcoming worry is by breathing deeply and relaxing your hands and all your muscles.

The second tip is to shift your mindset and stop thinking about the "Why Me?" and start thinking "Why NOT me?" Why shouldn't you be successful? Ron's boss and team members didn't hate him. On the contrary, they (most likely) appreciated the careful thought he put into his efforts to lead. But they do want decisions to be made.

Instead of being immobilized by ruminating about what you don't know others are thinking, give yourself a pep talk. You've done a LOT of great things! You are able to leap tall buildings in a single bound! You were the hero at the big game! You can fit FIVE cheeseburgers in your mouth at one time without choking! Remember those "glory moments" of triumph!

One more pointer when it comes to worry: make fear your bitch. After you quit worrying and get in the right mindset, nut up and take a step. If I take one step in the direction of what scares me, it in effect puts fear on the back of the motorcycle instead of it being the driver. Taking one small step also encourages me to take another. I'm either going to realize that there's nothing to be scared of, or I'm going to walk faster to get the hell out of there. Regardless, I'm back in control.

We all have to face fears all the time. We can either hide under the blankets, suck our thumb and wait for Mommy to come OR you can take the risk. There is no reward without risk. Do yourself and your team a favor and quit worrying. Step out; if you do, your team will too.

Another way I get in my own way is by living in the past and holding on to resentments. That serves nothing and no one, especially me. I'm thankful for all that I've gone through in my life. I'm the sum of all my experiences. I wouldn't want to go through some of that crap again but, in the end, I'm wiser for the wear and a better person because I went through it. Holding on to resentment is like taking poison and hoping the other person dies (as the saying goes).

Whether you've ever read the Bible or not, there is a passage in the book of Matthew when Jesus' disciples ask him how many times they should forgive their brother. He answered, "No, not seven times…but seventy times seven!" That's what I keep in mind when dealing with others. Knowing that we all are in the same boat and that we have all hard time letting go of blame and resentment actually helps me to release it. You can forgive and move on and get rid of the hurtful crap that weighs you down.

Feeling bitter interferes with your body's hormonal and immune systems, according to Carsten Wrosch, an associate professor of psychology at Concordia University in Montreal. Studies have shown that bitter, angry people have higher blood pressure and heart rate and are more likely to die of heart disease and other illnesses. I don't want to go like that, do you?

> STUDIES OF BRAIN SCANS SHOW THAT THE EMOTIONAL CENTERS OF THE LIMBIC SYSTEM LIGHT UP WHEN WE CONSIDER FORGIVING. (THAT'S A GOOD THING.)

Forgiving and letting go doesn't mean you accept or agree with what happened; nor does it even have to involve the other person. Forgiving is something you do for you, and it helps you step out of your own way and get past the crap.

Dr. Andrea Brandt wrote in *Psychology Today* some simple steps on how to forgive.

1. Think about the incident that angered you. Accept that it happened. Accept how you felt about it and how it made you react.

2. Acknowledge the growth you experienced as a result of what happened. What did it make you learn about yourself, or about your needs and boundaries? Not only did you survive the incident, perhaps you grew from it.

3. Now think about the other person. ALL human beings are flawed. When you were hurt, the other person was trying to

have a need met. What do you think this need was and why did the person go about it in such a hurtful way?

4. Finally, decide whether or not you want to tell the other person that you have forgiven him or her. If you decide not to express forgiveness directly, then do it on your own. Say the words, "I forgive you," aloud.

> # RESENTMENT IS CRAP. IT DOES NOT MAKE YOU A BETTER LEADER OR A BIGGER PERSON. LET IT GO.

Life is not always a bed of roses. We all know that. Why should we even expect there to never be any road bumps or challenges? That is unrealistic. Life is sometimes full of crap and crappy people. As always, we have a choice to make. Don't be your own barrier. Take the pledge to be a resilient leader. Lead yourself first. Step out of your own way and make a habit of getting past the crap.

GET PAST THE CRAP!

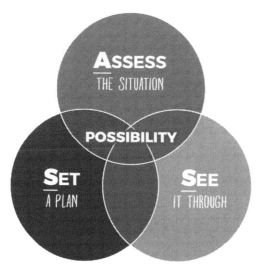

ASSESS YOUR CURRENT SITUATION

Where are you on the Craptometer scale?

LEVEL 1	LEVEL 2	LEVEL 3	LEVEL 4
Everything is **CRAPTASTIC!**	Same Old **CRAP**	**CRAP** is getting **HEAVY**	My Life is **CRAP**

ARE YOU WILLING TO TAKE THE PLEDGE TO GET PAST YOUR CRAP?

- Are you in your own way?
- What internal dialogue are you telling yourself?

SET A PLAN

1. What are three things you can tell yourself to help you get out of your own way?
2. What are you currently worried about? Is it real or perceived? Is it within your control?
3. Who do you need to forgive?
4. What small step can you take to get past your crap?

SEE IT THROUGH

Write down specific concrete actions:

Today, I will _____
_____.

This week, I will _____
_____.

This month, I will _____
_____.

WRITE DOWN YOUR POSSIBILITY:

CHAPTER 8

PUTTING IT ALL **TOGETHER** TO GET PAST THE CRAP

"I may not have gone where I intended to go, but I think I have ended up where I needed to be."
–Douglas Adams

How you handle your crap sandwich makes all the difference in your ability to get past it and move on…and, maybe learn something in the process.

Repeat after me:

I have a choice.

I can choose to let the crap control me or I can look for ways to take control.

When I have control, my stress decreases and I can see things more clearly.

When I can see things more clearly, I am better able to take action.

When I take action, I have more control.

When I have control, I can see things more clearly.

SO THE CYCLE GOES.

When I was a junior Sailor, I worked in personnel and, with that being the case, had to work in customer service. My boss was keen on us doing the best we could at whatever was in front of us, so he had us complete the Navy Customer Service Manual. I will never forget the words that popped up from the pages as I read: "When dealing with a customer issue, your attitude should say you can help them and your actions should say that you will help them."

Can and will. Two words that have very different meaning but two words that we use interchangeably many times. There are a lot of things that I can do. I can run a marathon. Will I? No (my knees are bad and, quite frankly, the only thing I like about running is stopping). I can jump from 14000 feet from an airplane. Will I? Yes, it was a rush the first time I did it and it will be a rush every time thereafter.

Putting everything together from this book is about your choice to implement can and will. What do you say? Are you game?

You can and will live by your purpose and stay focused on where you are going.

You can and will be a positive thinker and not let the carriers of the world pull you into more crap.

You can and will pay attention and not let the crap of taco body moments get the better of you.

You can and will be pliable and take the risks necessary to achieve great things.

You can and will practice happiness every day and not just when others are around.

You can and will play more and take yourself less seriously.

You can and will take the pledge to step out of your own way and succeed!

Does that sound like a tall order? It's absolutely doable and it's the best way to eat that sandwich. You can and will always choose Option 3 to get past the crap, lead yourself first, and be resilient!

It was Cesare Pavese who said, "We don't remember days, but we remember moments." That's all we have in this life are a bunch of discombobulated moments. We have moments where we are living life, all is good. But we also have moments when the storm that is upon us is overwhelming, we have the negative brain, and the sandwich that has been handed to us seems too much. But the nice thing is that we also have moments of choice. We can choose how we act and interact with our environment.

This same poet and author Pavese also said, "If you wish to travel far and fast, travel light. Take off all your envies, jealousies, unforgiveness, selfishness and fears." As a leader, you want to be the best you can be. Implement the seven steps laid out here

(Purpose, Positive Thinking, Paying Attention, Being Pliable, Practice, Play and Pledge) and you can be that resilient leader who stresses less and enjoys more. It's up to you. You don't need any more studies, science or stats. It all comes down to practical application. Your time is now.

You can choose to stay stuck in the crap, or you can choose to do something different. You don't have to make life any harder than it needs to be. You can make it easier on yourself and everyone around you. You can choose to get past the crap today, tomorrow, and every day. As Ralph Waldo Emerson said, "The only person you are destined to become is the person you decide to be."

It's good to read the words of Stephen Covey: "I am not a product of my circumstances. I am a product of my decisions." What is your decision?

Choose to face your challenges head on. Choose Option 3. Be the resilient leader that leads yourself first, bounces back, and gets shit done. Be smart. Be someone who can ASS – Assess the situation, Set a plan and See it through. That's where possibility happens. You will never regret it.

ACKNOWLEDGEMENTS

Nothing happens on its own. I'm grateful for all of the experiences I've had in my life and of all the people who have impacted me. This project came about due to some strange circumstances in my health but, in looking back, it came at just the right time and I need to thank a few people that have helped me along the way.

Sandra Lutz, my mother, for always expanding my horizons, loving me unconditionally, and not selling me to the circus when I was a child.

Eugene Lutz, my father, for being a great father, role model, and instilling in me a great sense of humor and work ethic.

Gwen, my bride, for being continually supportive and pushing me perpetually outside my comfort zone.

Matt, my brother, for always listening to me bitch, always making me laugh and giving me great stories to tell.

Derek, my nephew, for his poop illustrations in this book.

Kelly Epperson, my book coach, for making me sound smarter than I really am and being a positive force in completing this book.

My four kids (Victoria, Christian, Abby and Ben) for giving me reason to get past all of life's crap. I'm a lucky guy to have children as great as you. (Special thanks to Christian for proofreading.)

All of the leaders I've had the pleasure to work with, learn from, and took the time to invest themselves in me.

A special thanks to Dr. Alan Licup for working the Easter holiday and for saving my life. You've seen parts of me no one else has (or wanted to). You're okay for an Air Force guy.

ABOUT THE AUTHOR

Lieutenant Commander Chip Lutz, USN(Ret), MSEd, CSP, is the President and Founder of Unconventional Leader, LLC, and has three decades of solid leadership experience. A retired Navy Officer, he has had two command tours and also served as the Director of Security for Naval District Washington, DC during September 11th, 2001. In that capacity, he was responsible for the safety and security of 25,000 people on six different Naval Installations in the National Capital Region during one of our country's most trying times.

A seasoned educator and trainer, he is currently adjunct faculty for two different universities and has taught over 20 different classes in leadership, management, human resource development, and organizational behavior. Chip is the author of 5 books, been published in Security Management Magazine, and has had numerous articles on teamwork and leadership published in Zig Ziglar's Weekly Newsletter.

Chip has earned the Certified Speaking Professional® (CSP) designation. Conferred by the National Speakers Association, the CSP is the speaking profession's international measure of professional platform competence. Only 12 percent of the 5,000 + speakers worldwide, who belong to the Global Speakers Federation, currently hold this professional designation.

Chip is a leader who has been there, done that, and has the uniform to prove it! He works with leaders who WANT to lead better, get more done, and leave a legacy. He is where theory meets application.

You can connect with Chip on almost ALL social media platforms.

Listen to his podcast at **www.leadershiphappyhour.com.**

Visit **www.unconventionalleader.com** to sign up for his monthly newsletter and keep up to date on how to bring Chip in to speak to your organization, work with your team, or coach you to become an even more resilient leader.

Made in the USA
Columbia, SC
02 February 2021